ILLUSTRATIONS BY KARLIE ALTHERR

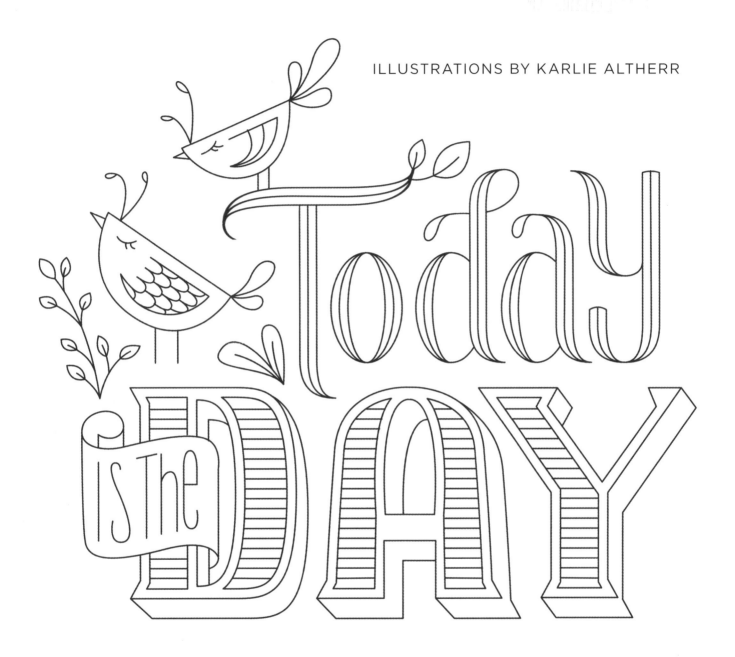

# Today Is the Day

## A COLORING BOOK FOR INSPIRED LIVING

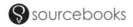 sourcebooks

# INTRODUCTION

For several years, I worked in a highly competitive job and felt stuck in the grind. I longed to create projects that would provide inspiration both for me and for other people. Simply put, I wanted to make art that would make people happy. Now I run a stationery business, and every day I get to create art that lifts people up when the world wants to tear them down.

My personal motto is to "be a lighthouse." When I illustrate a quote or a hand-lettered piece of art, I put great care into adding unique detail into each letter to make sure the impact is immediate and resonates with the viewer. I hope this book resonates with you in some way, and inspires you to be a lighthouse, to stand tall and shine your light on those around you.

—Karlie Altherr

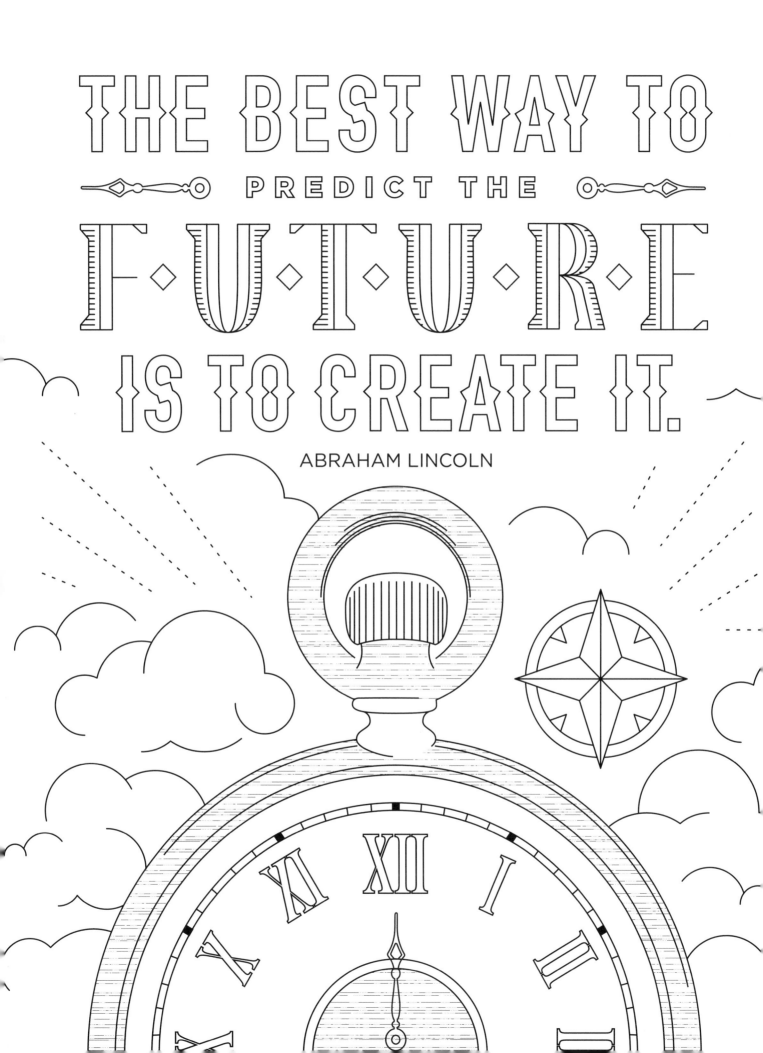

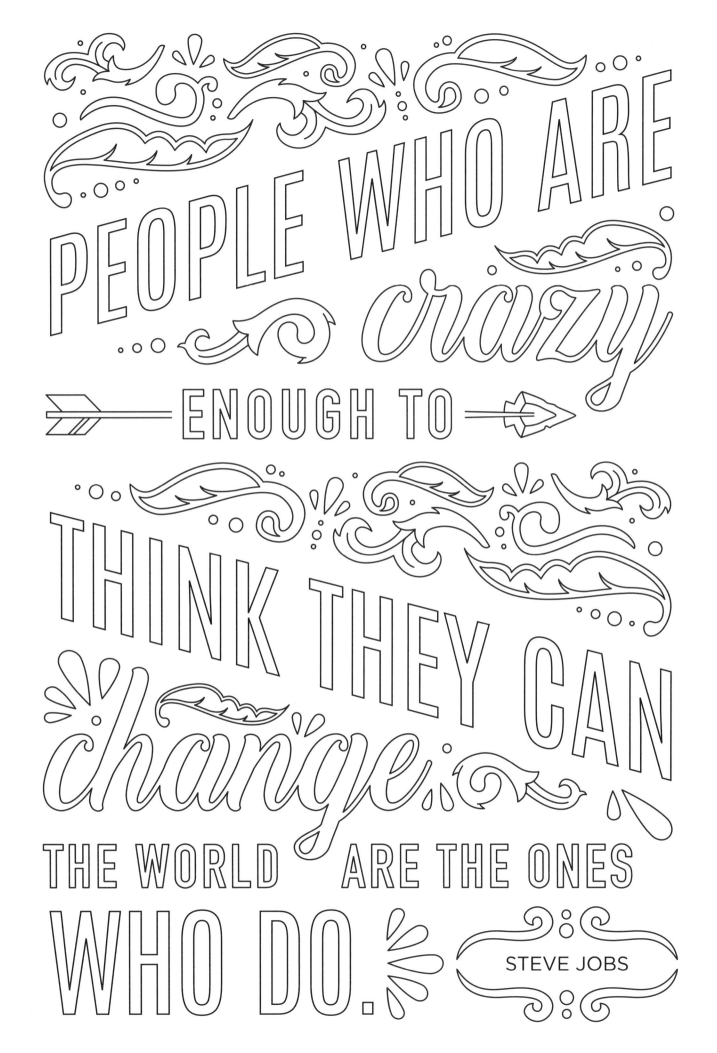

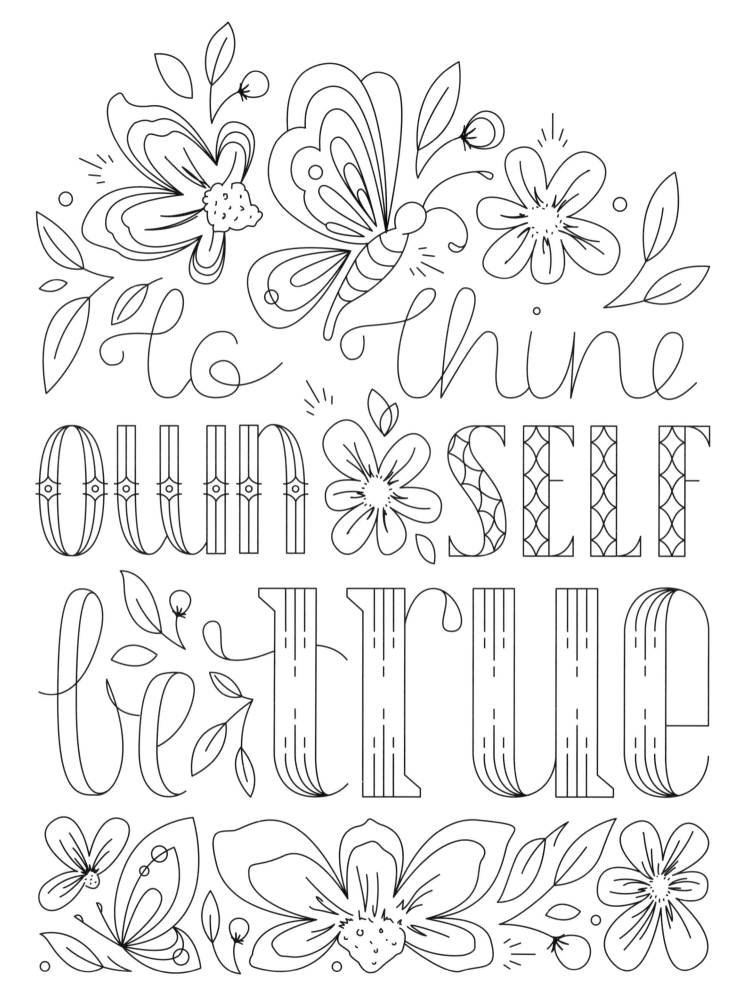

To thine own self be true

WILLIAM SHAKESPEARE

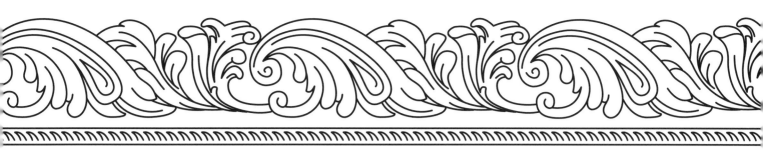

SUCCESS IS NOT THE KEY TO HAPPINESS

HAPPINESS IS THE KEY TO SUCCESS

ALBERT SCHWEITZER

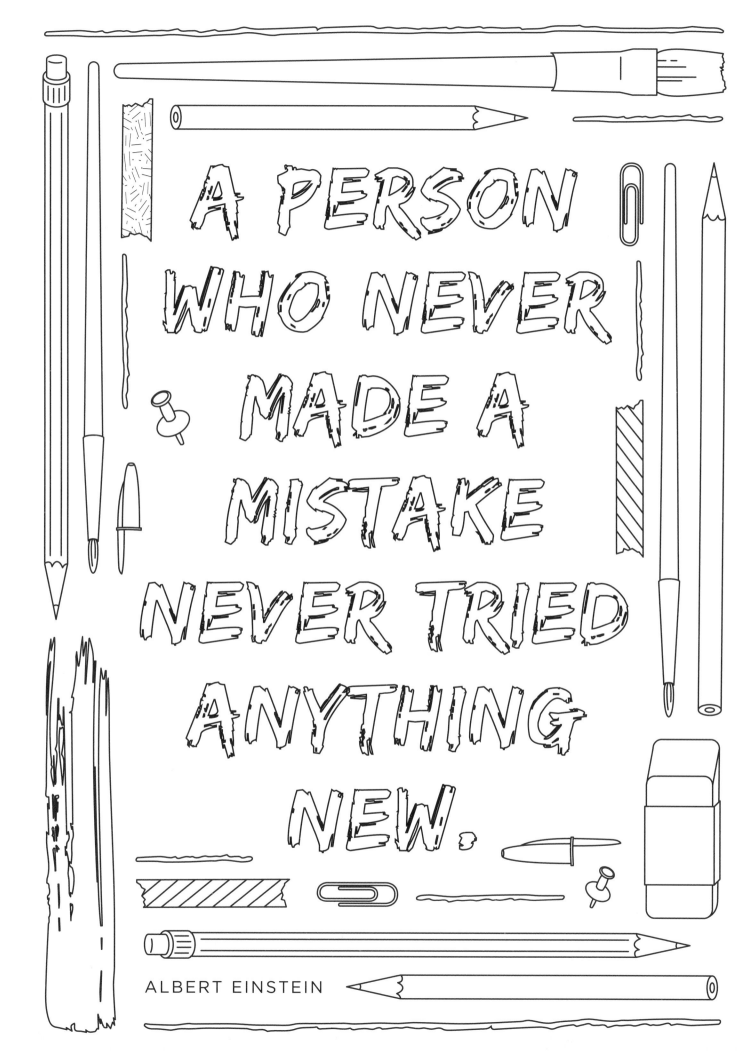

A PERSON WHO NEVER MADE A MISTAKE NEVER TRIED ANYTHING NEW.

ALBERT EINSTEIN

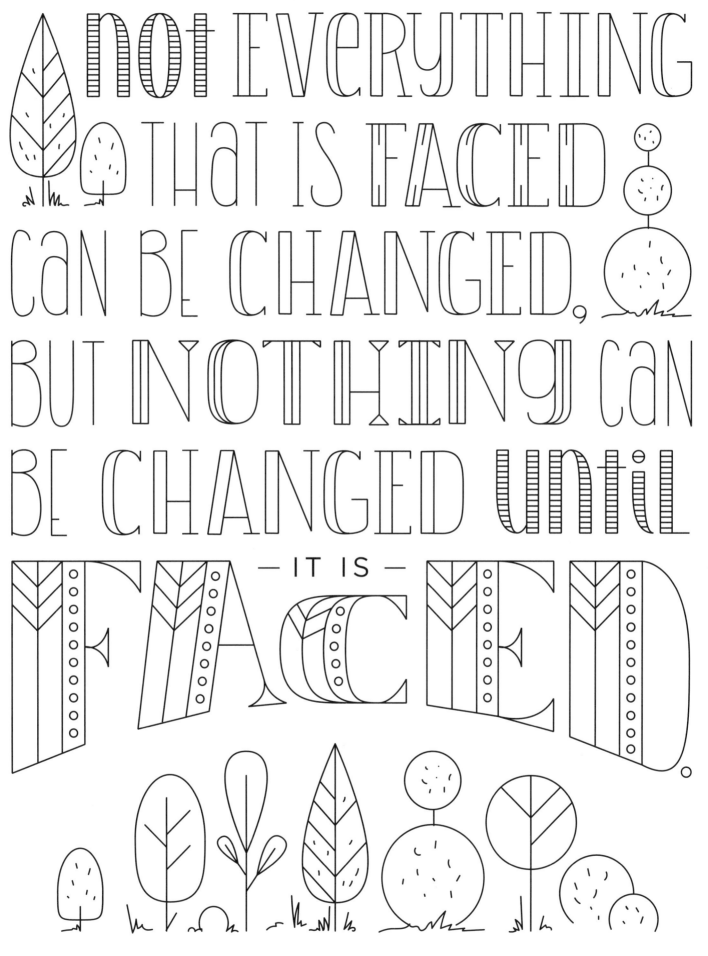

not everything that is faced can be changed, but nothing can be changed until —IT IS— FACED.

— JAMES BALDWIN —

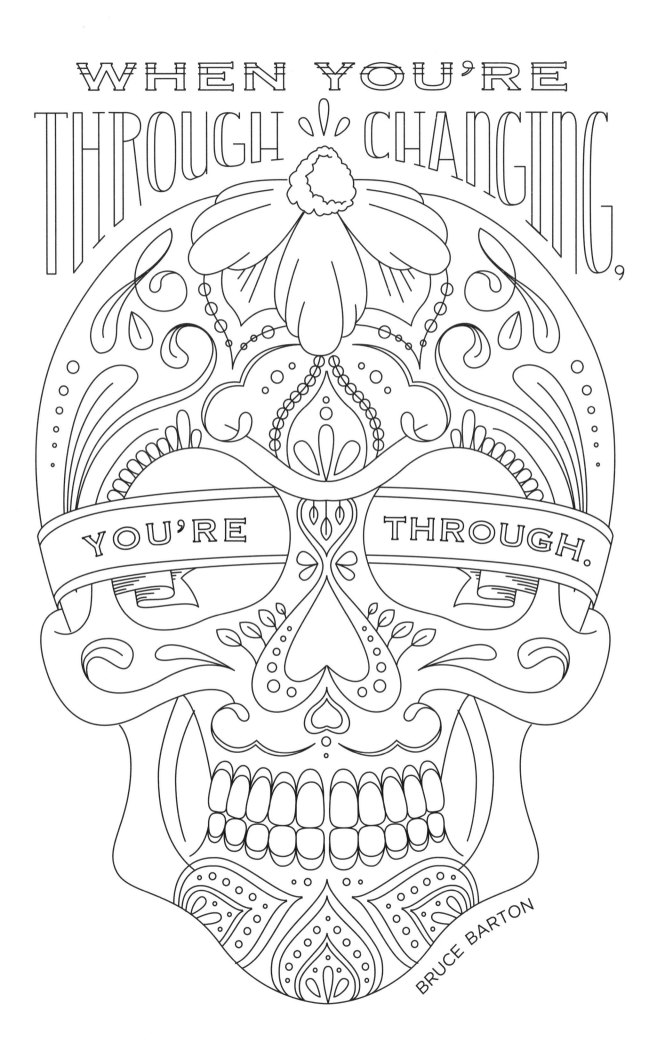

IT IS NEVER TOO LATE TO BE WHO YOU MIGHT HAVE BEEN.

GEORGE ELIOT

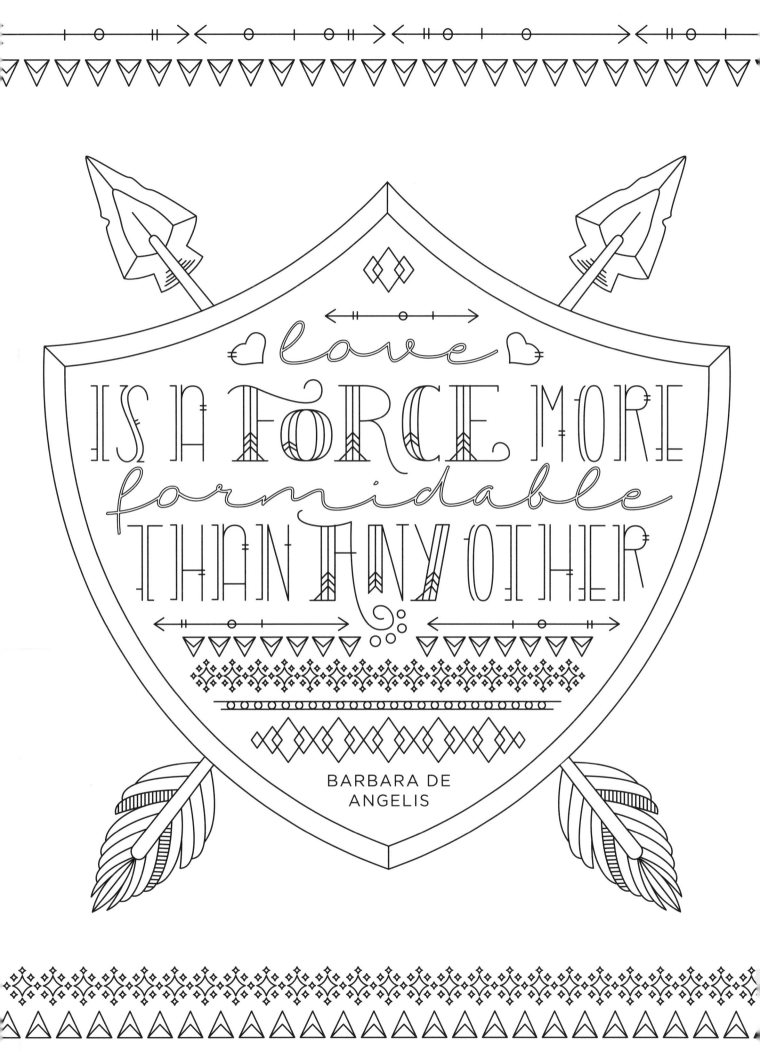

love is a force more formidable than any other

BARBARA DE ANGELIS

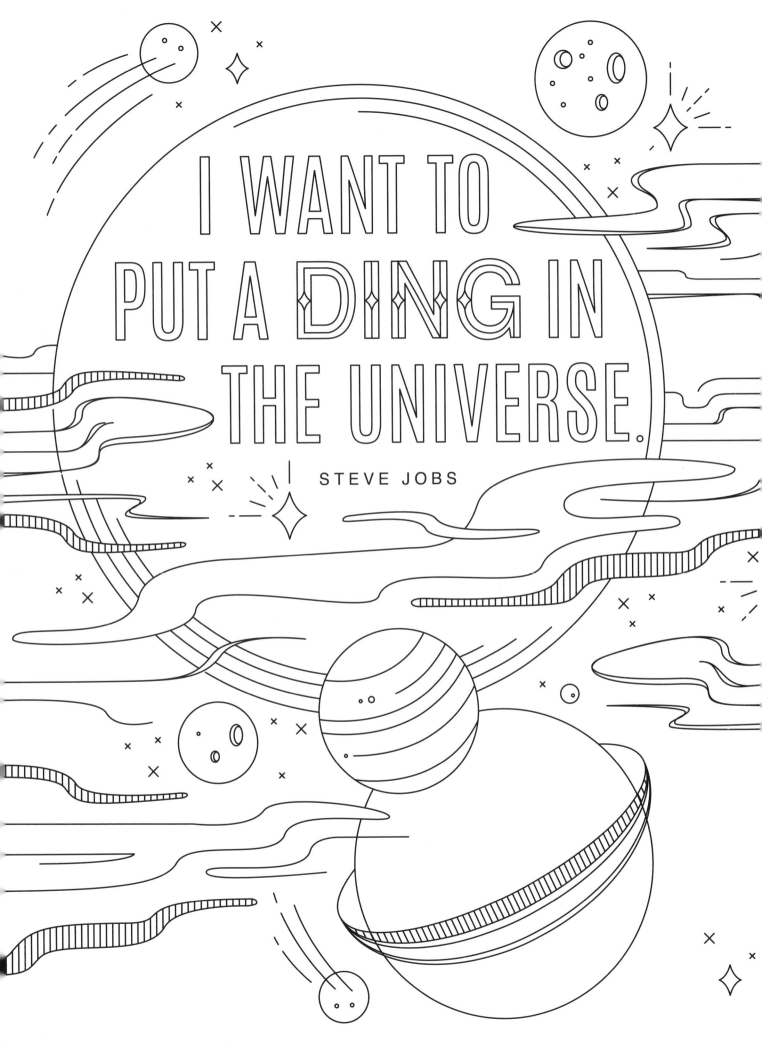

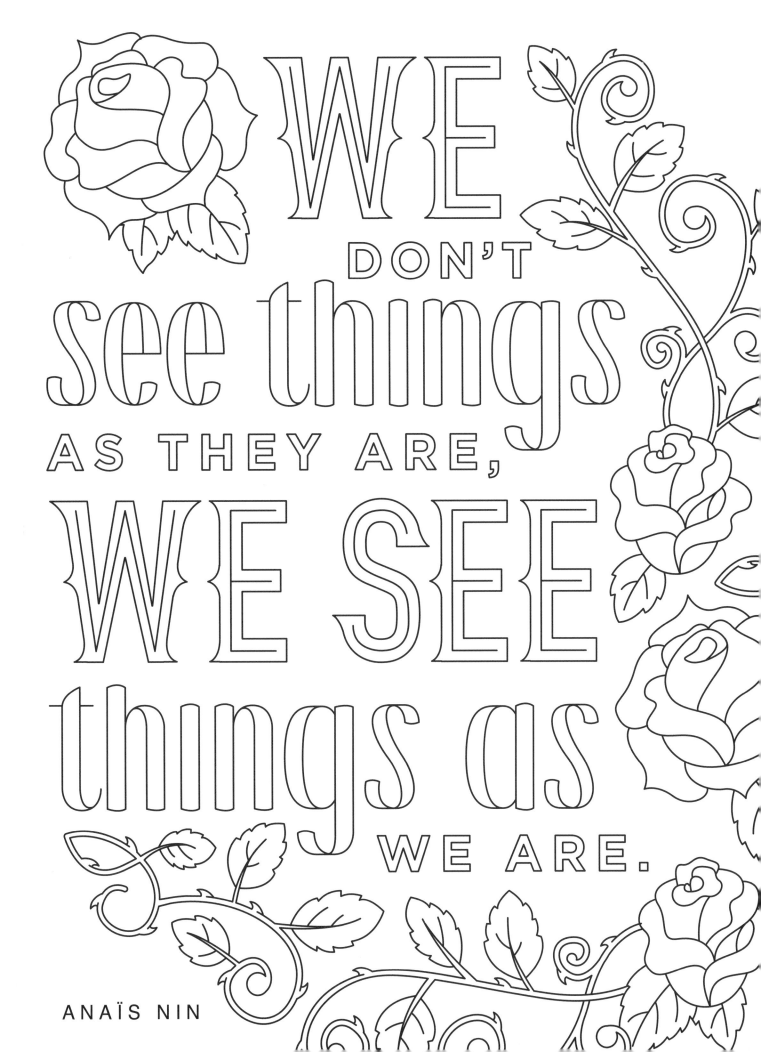

WE DON'T see things AS THEY ARE, WE SEE things as WE ARE.

ANAÏS NIN

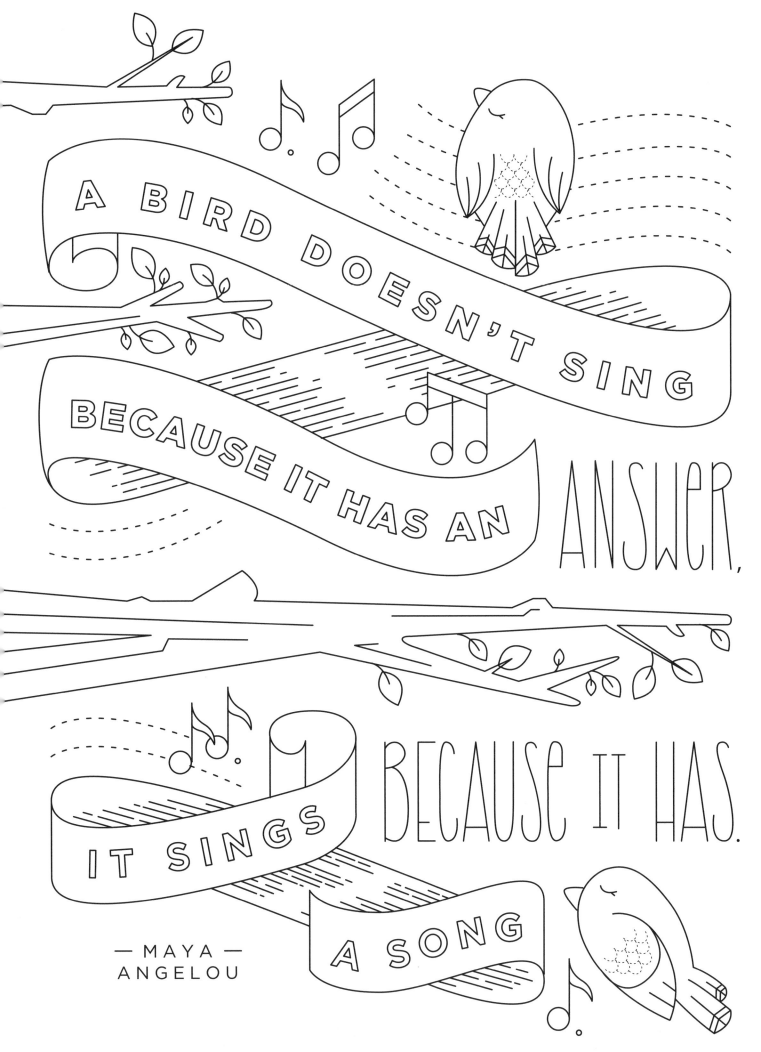

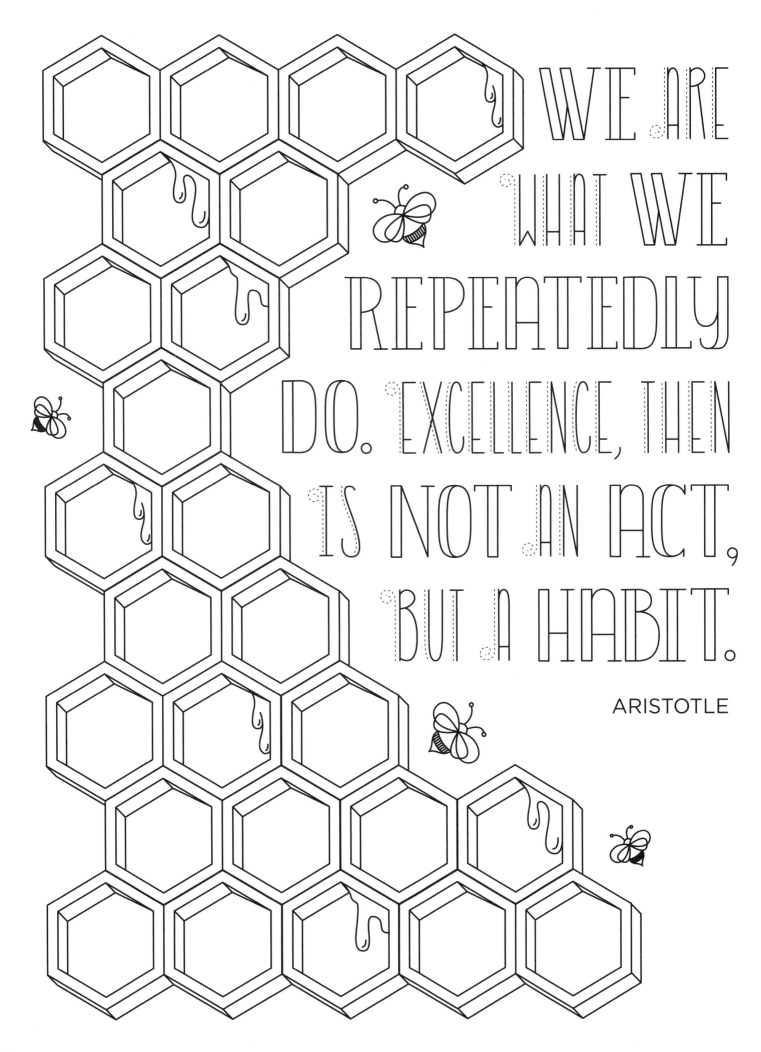

WE ARE WHAT WE REPEATEDLY DO. EXCELLENCE, THEN IS NOT AN ACT, BUT A HABIT.

ARISTOTLE

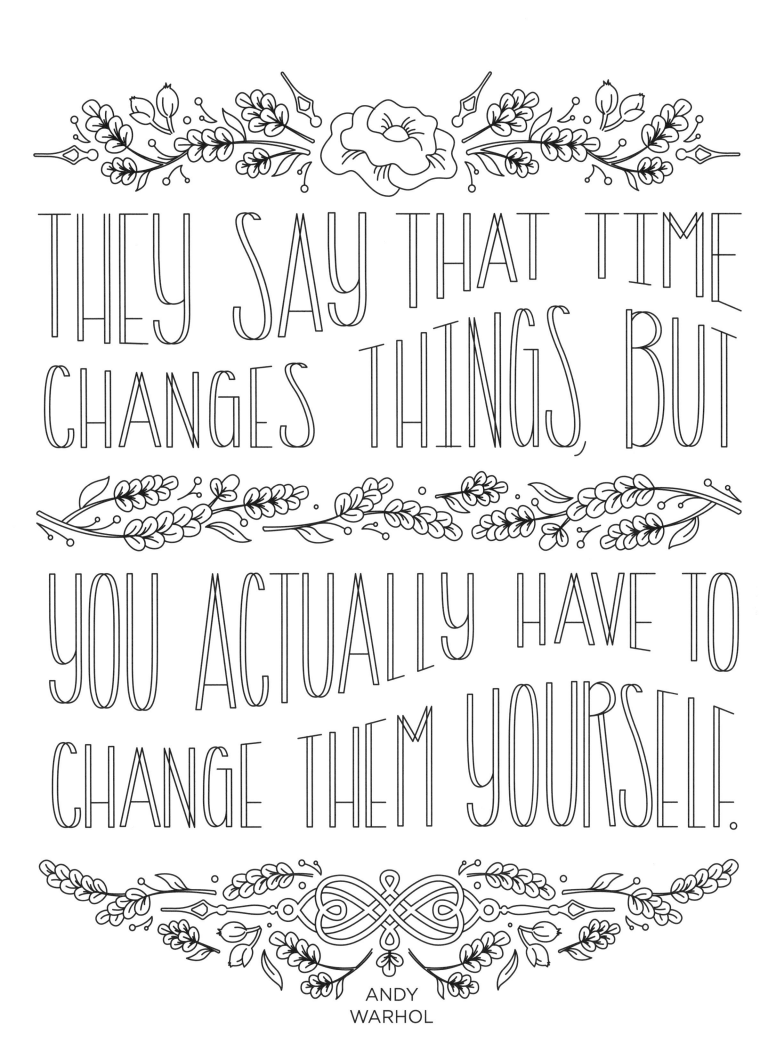

THEY SAY THAT TIME CHANGES THINGS, BUT YOU ACTUALLY HAVE TO CHANGE THEM YOURSELF.

ANDY WARHOL

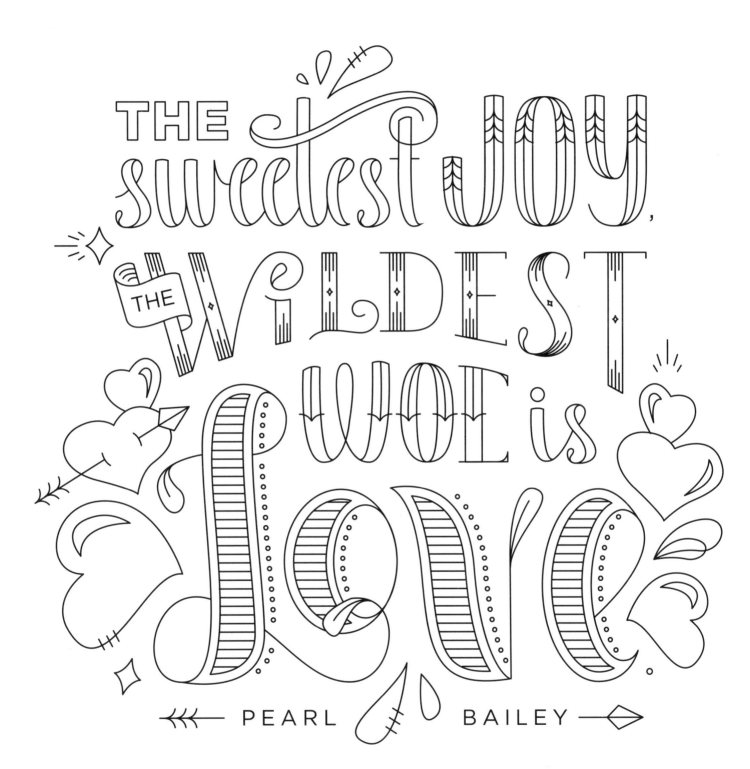

THE sweetest JOY, the WILDEST WOE is love.

— PEARL BAILEY →

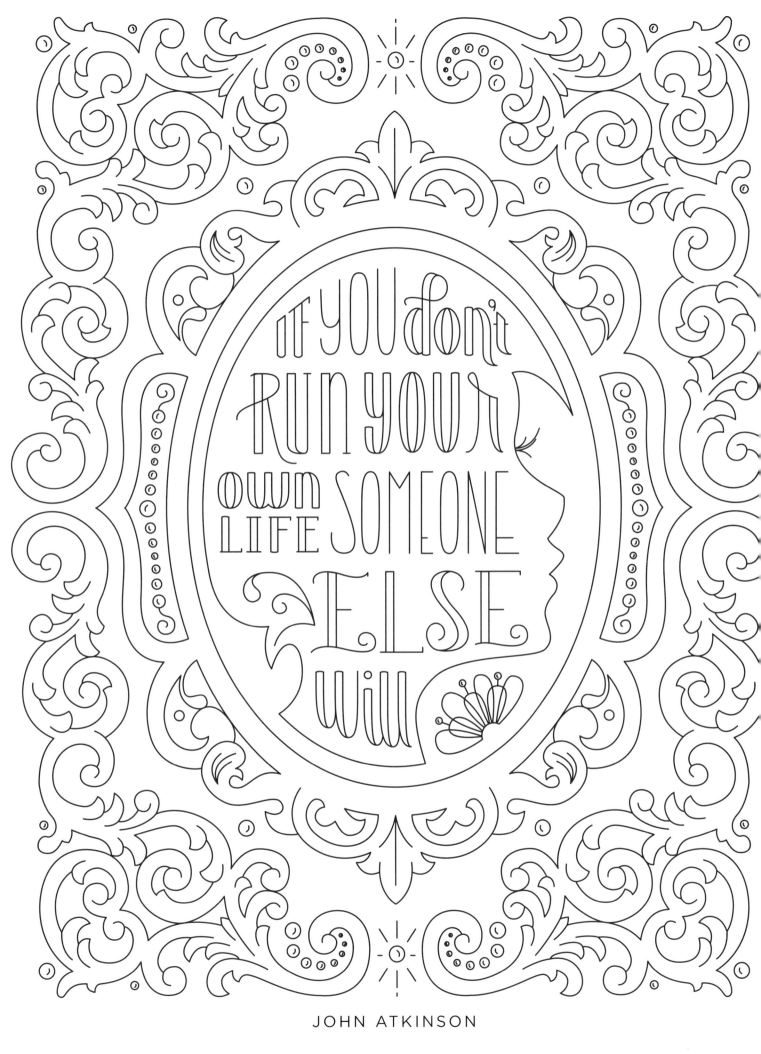

If you don't run your own life someone else will

JOHN ATKINSON

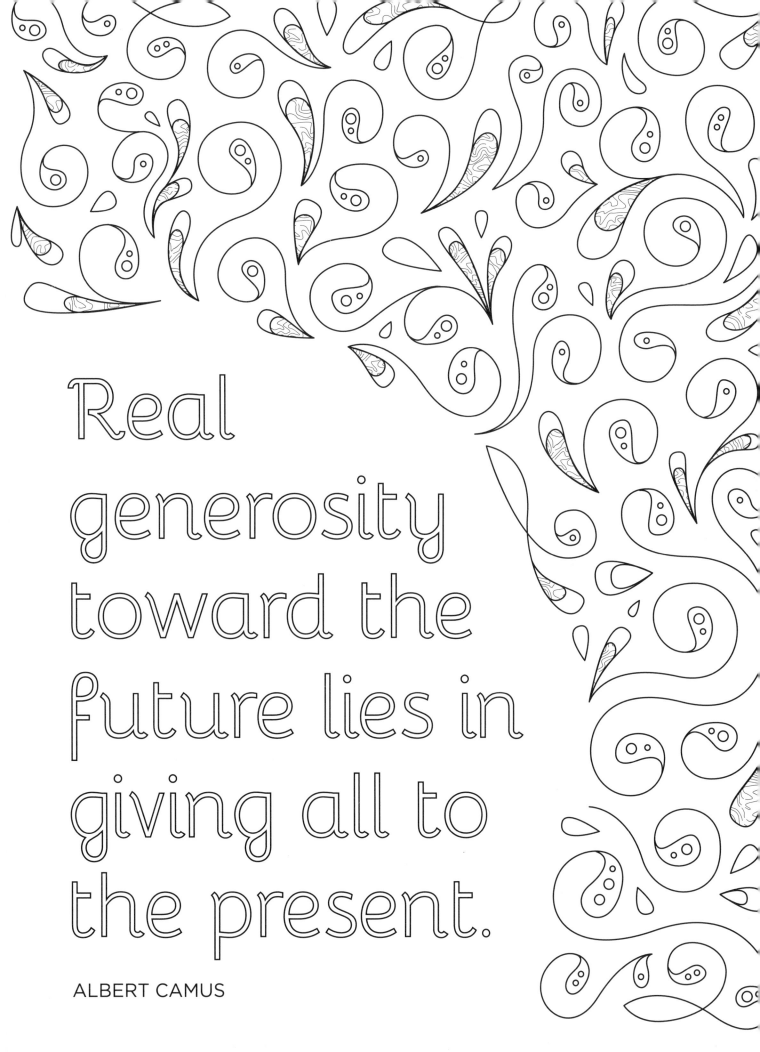

Real generosity toward the future lies in giving all to the present.

ALBERT CAMUS

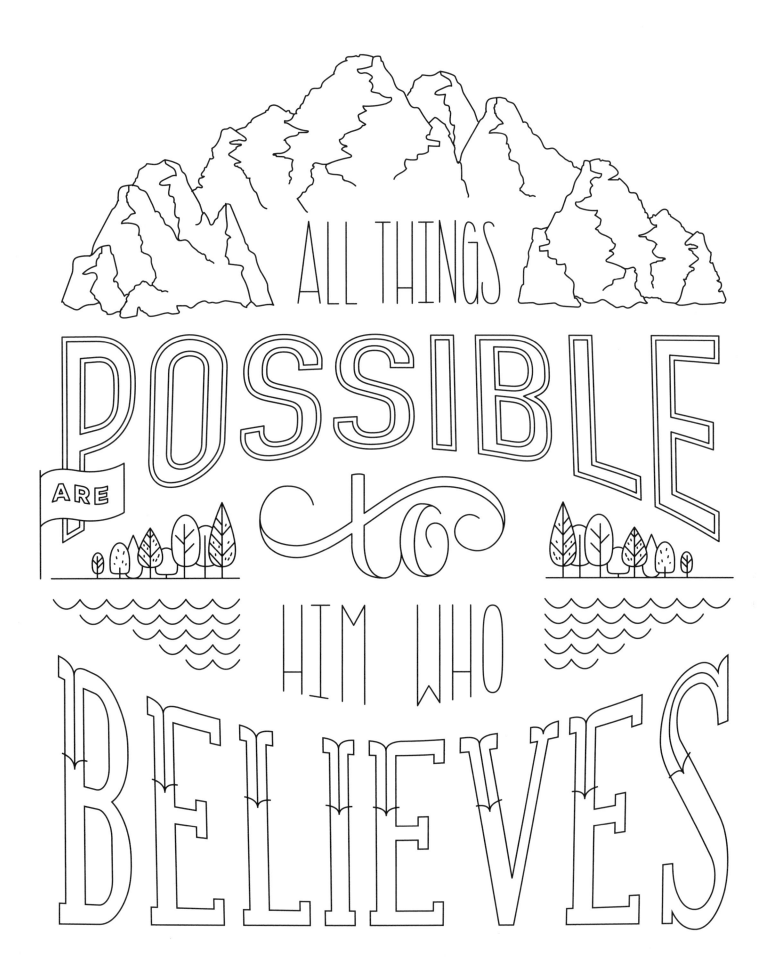

ALL THINGS POSSIBLE ARE to HIM WHO BELIEVES

MARK 9:23

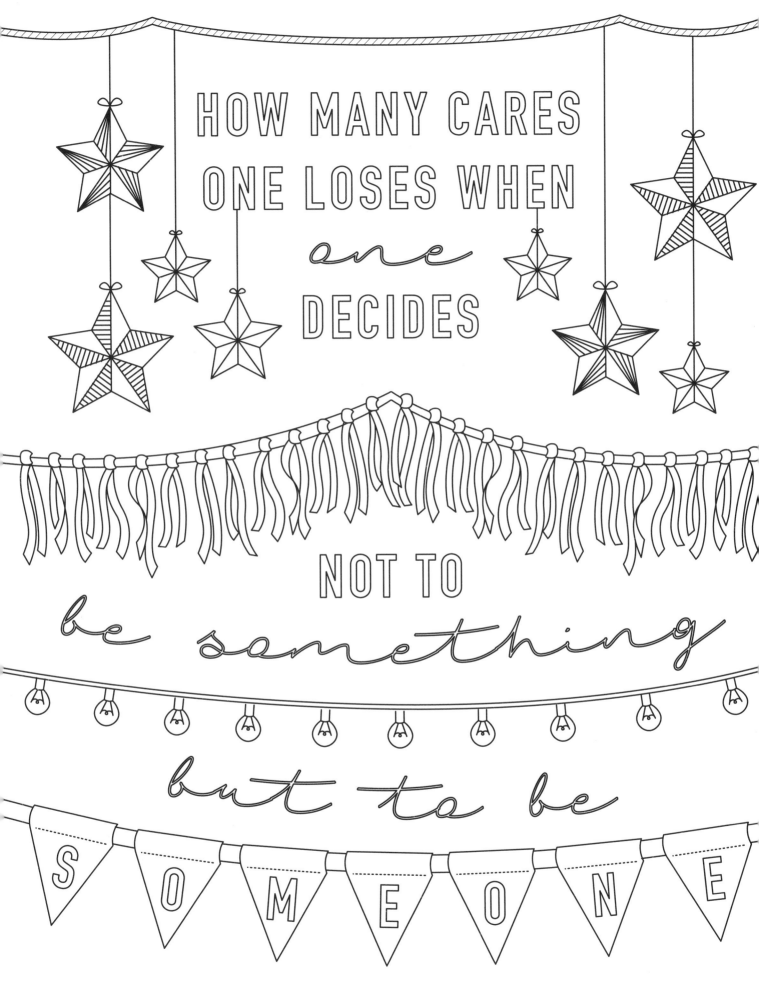

HOW MANY CARES
ONE LOSES WHEN
*one*
DECIDES

NOT TO

*be something*

*but to be*

SOMEONE

COCO CHANEL

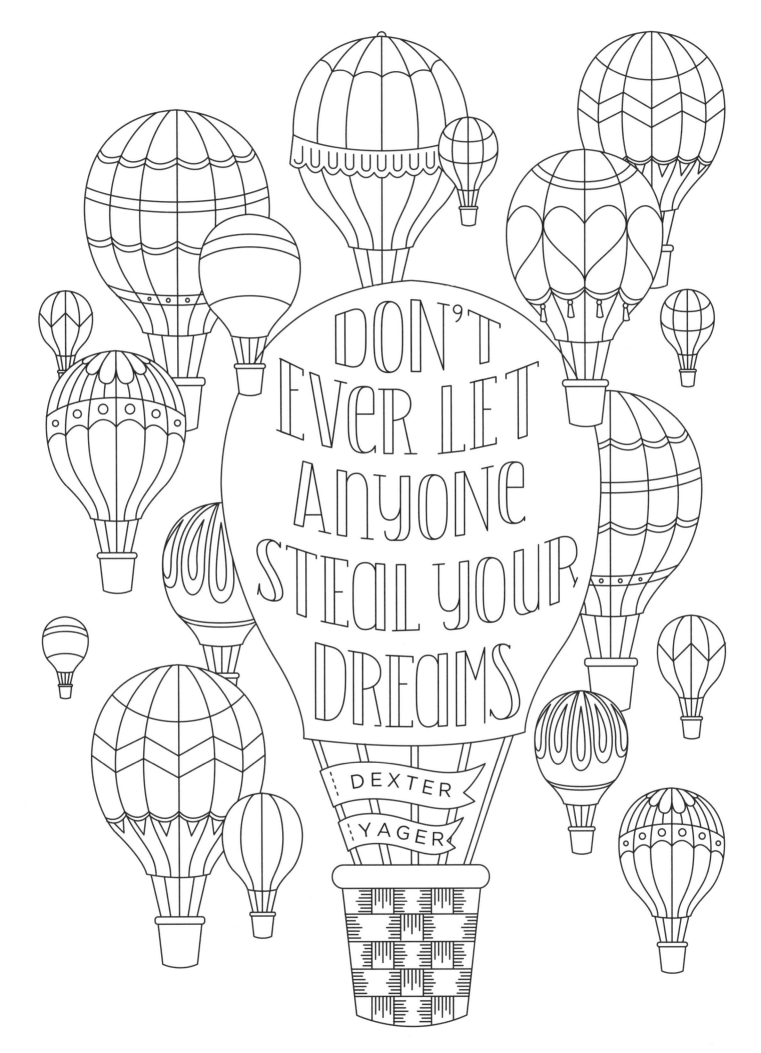

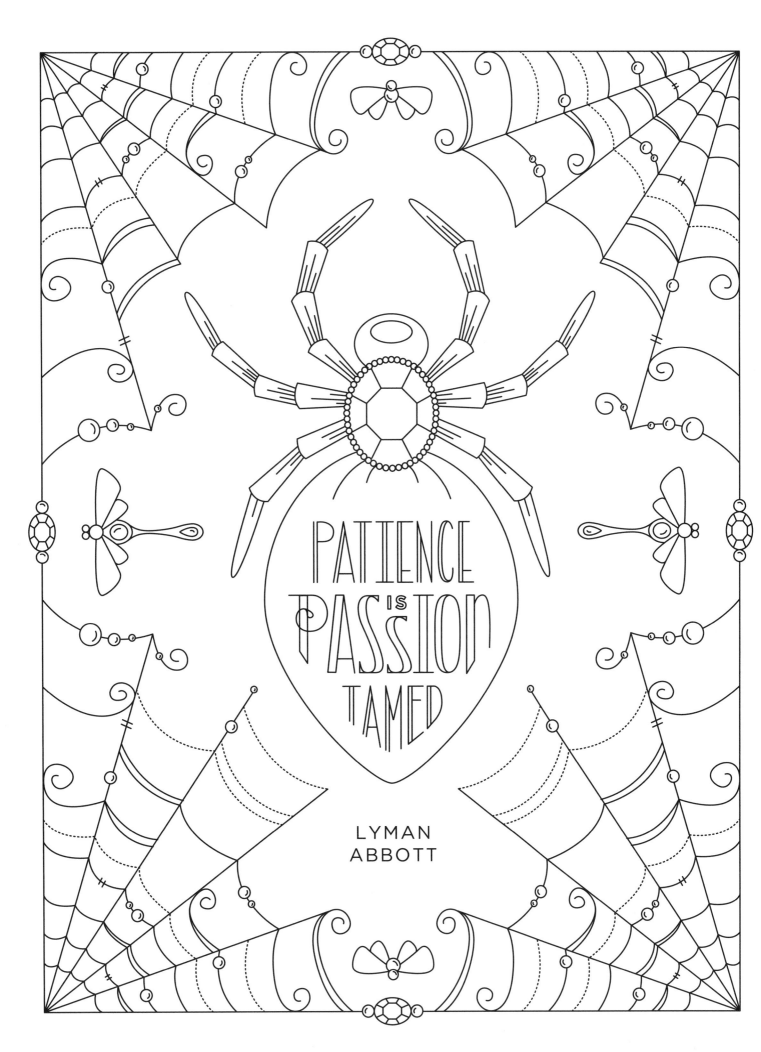

PATIENCE PASSION IS TAMED

LYMAN ABBOTT

You Can Give

WITHOUT LOVING,

BUT YOU CANNOT

LOVE

WITHOUT giving.

AMY CARMICHAEL

I
AM NOT
WHAT HAPPENED
TO ME, I AM WHAT
I CHOOSE TO
BECOME.

CARL JUNG

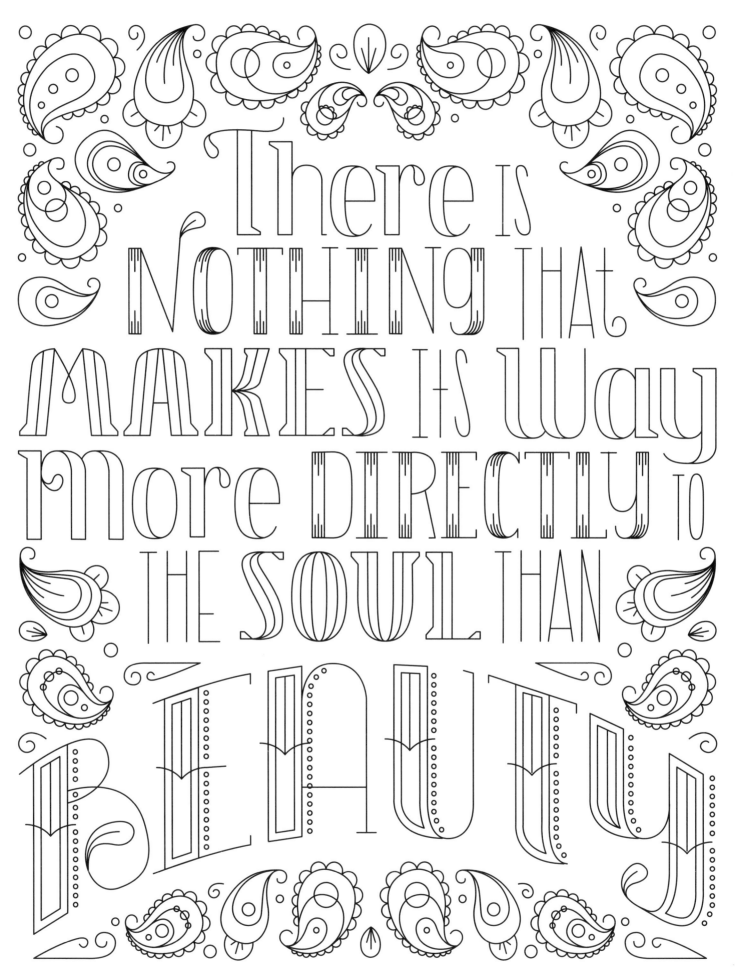

There is
NOTHING THAT
MAKES ITS WAY
MORE DIRECTLY TO
THE SOUL THAN
BEAUTY

JOSEPH ADDISON

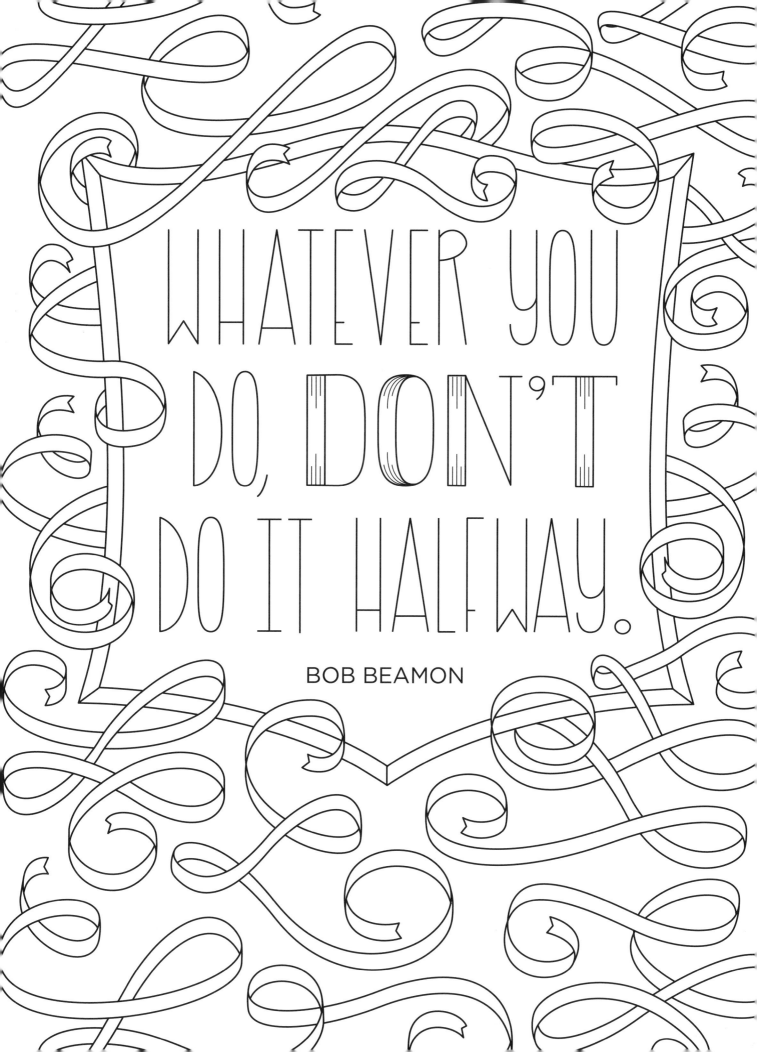

WHATEVER YOU DO, DON'T DO IT HALFWAY.

BOB BEAMON

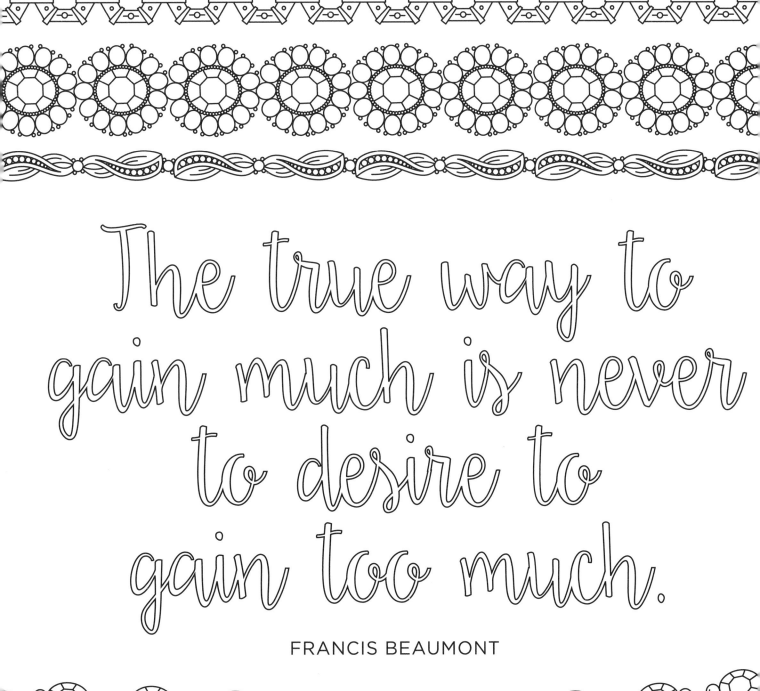

The true way to gain much is never to desire to gain too much.

FRANCIS BEAUMONT

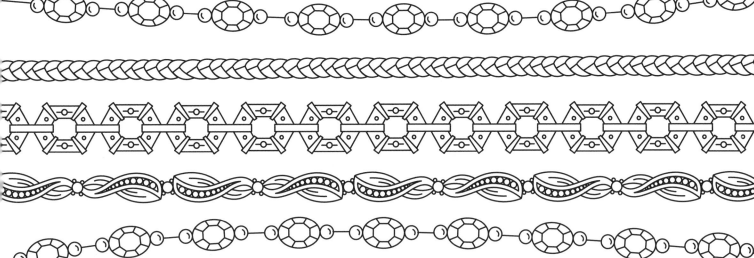

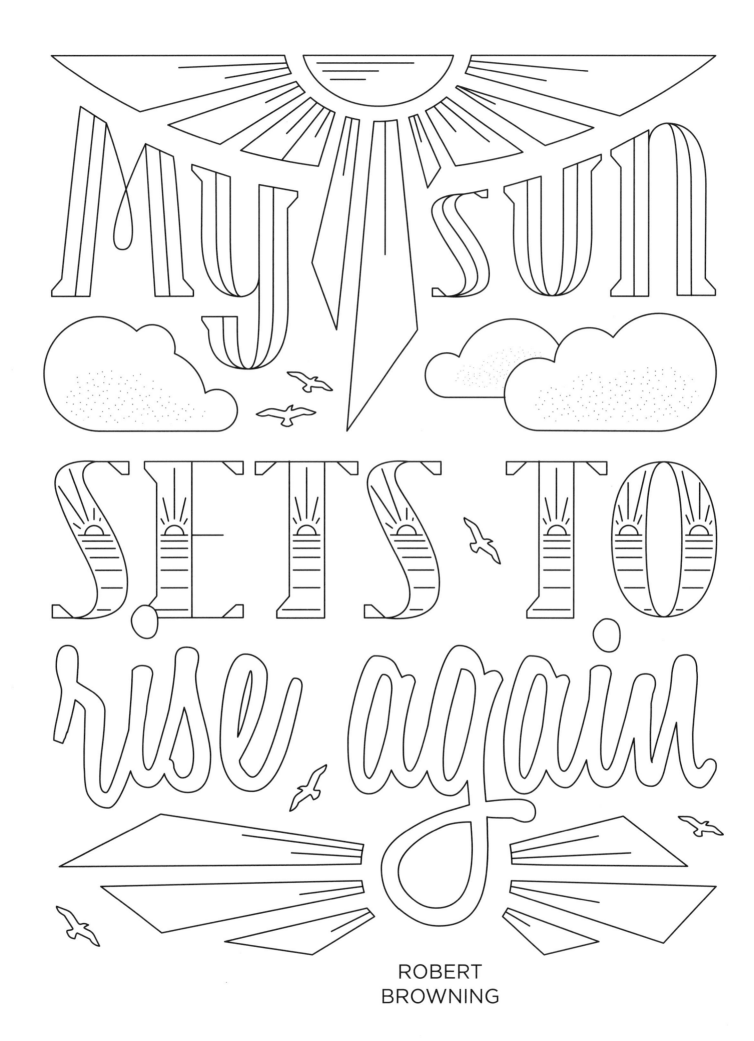

ROBERT
BROWNING

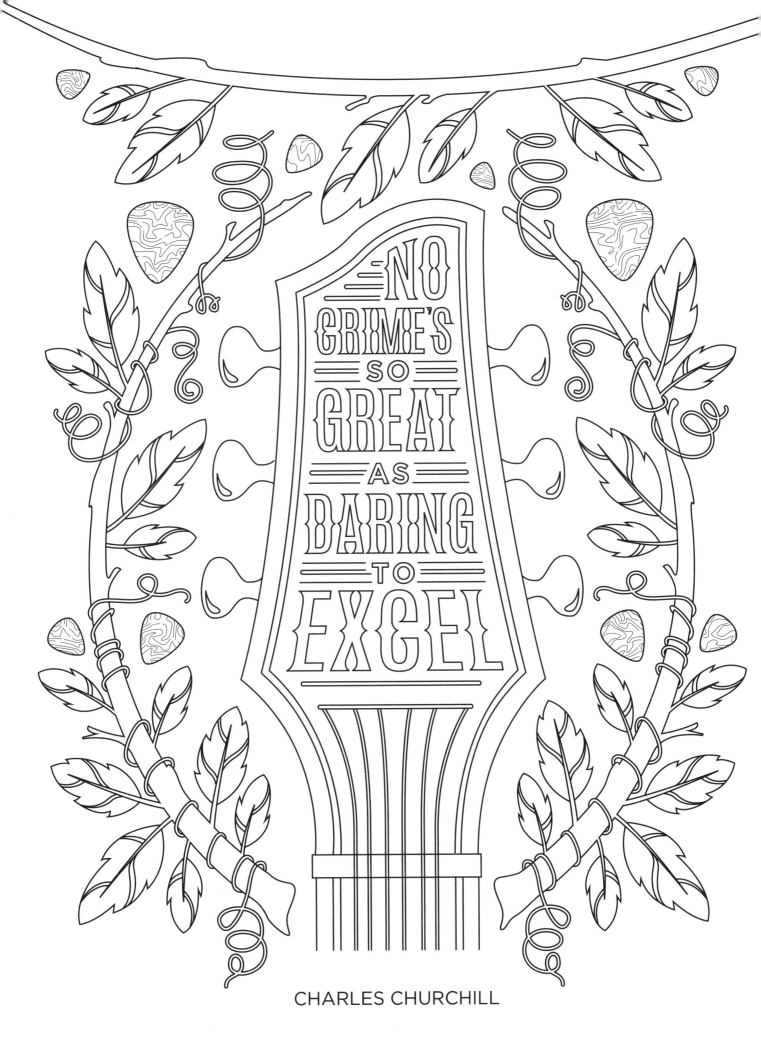

NO CRIME'S SO GREAT AS DARING TO EXCEL

CHARLES CHURCHILL

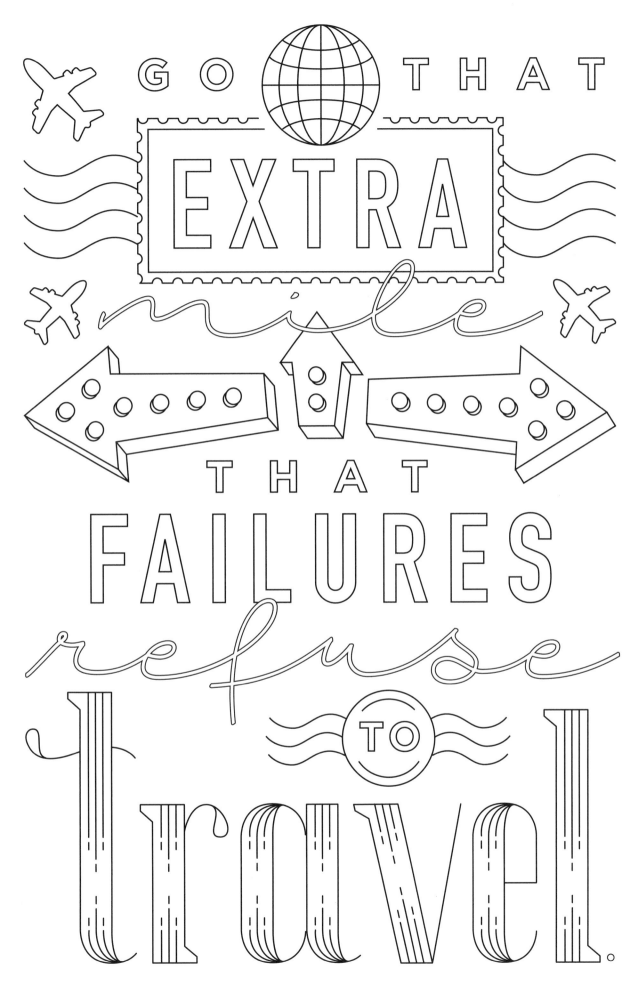

GO THAT EXTRA *mile* THAT FAILURES *refuse* TO *travel.*

MARY KAY ASH

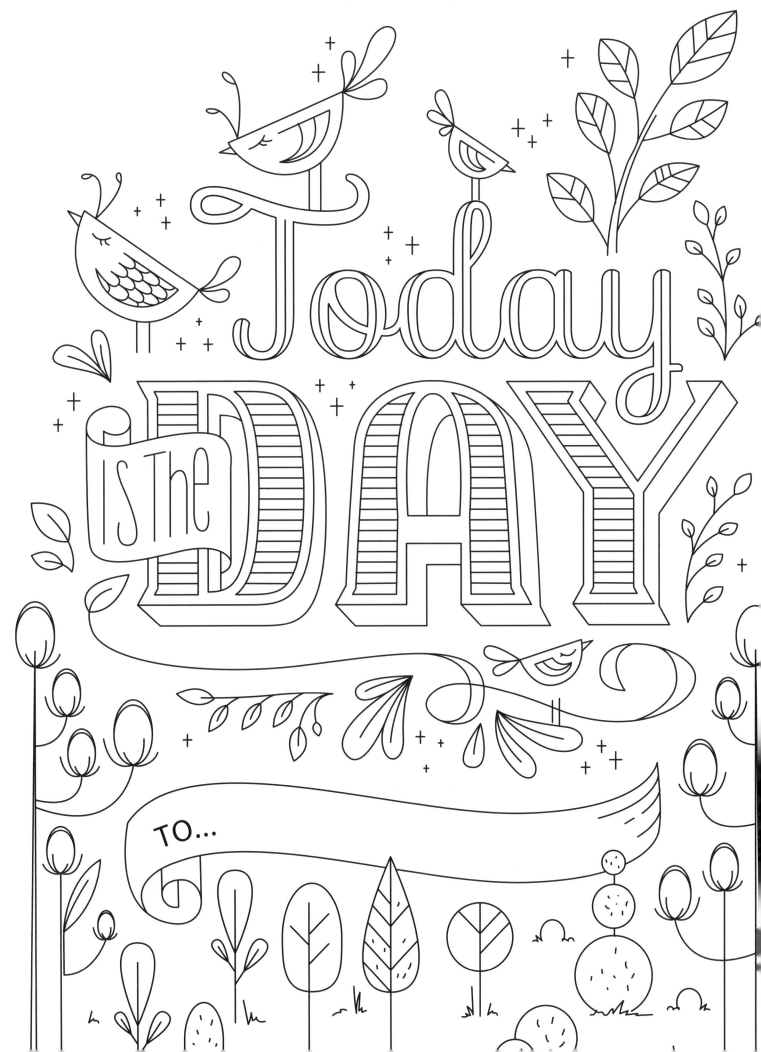

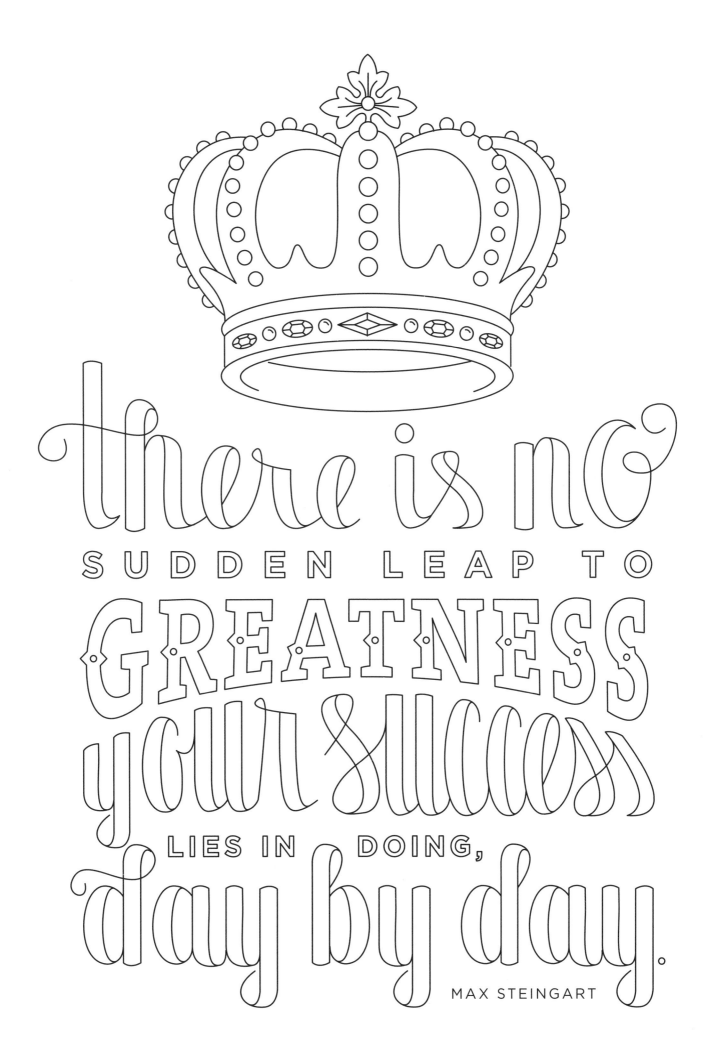

there is no
SUDDEN LEAP TO
GREATNESS
your success
LIES IN DOING,
day by day.

MAX STEINGART

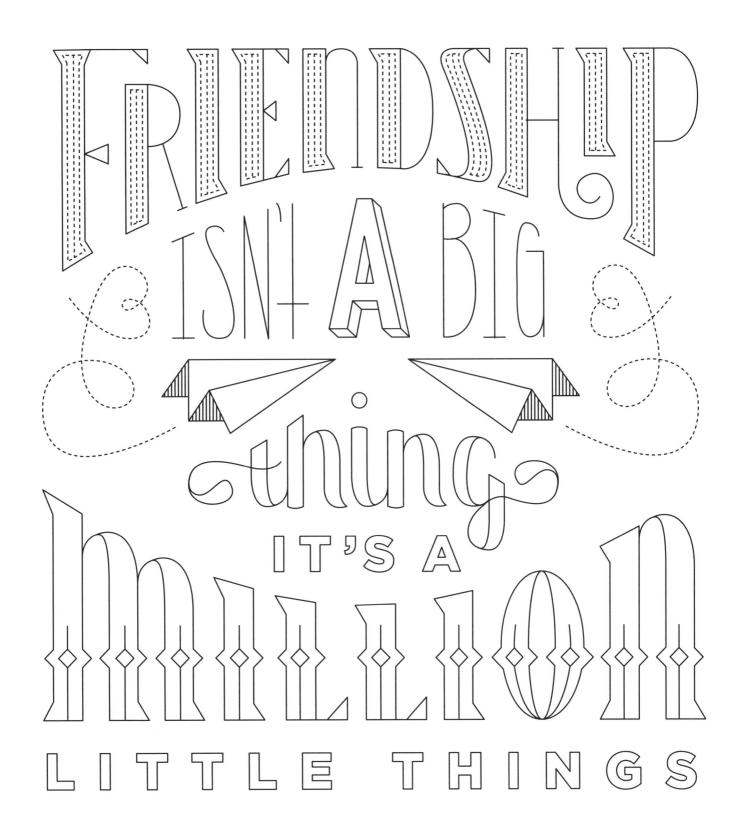

FRIENDSHIP ISN'T A BIG thing IT'S A million LITTLE THINGS

----- ANONYMOUS -----

YOU MUST BE THE CHANGE you wish TO SEE IN the world.

MAHATMA GANDHI

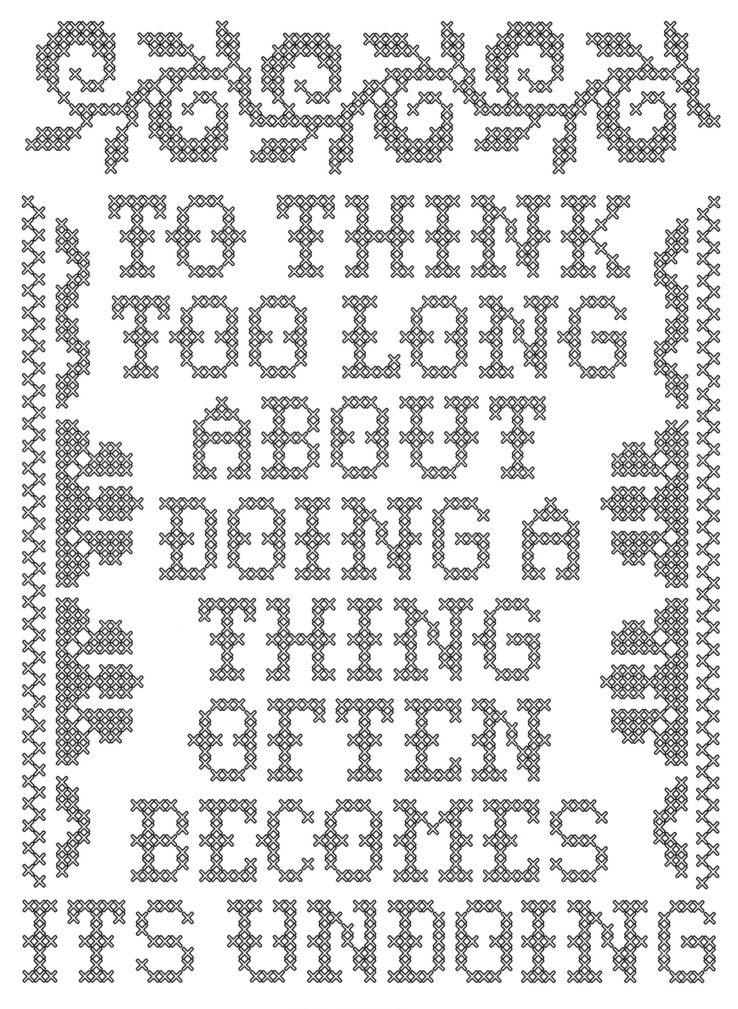

TO THINK TOO LONG ABOUT DOING A THING OFTEN BECOMES ITS UNDOING

EVA YOUNG

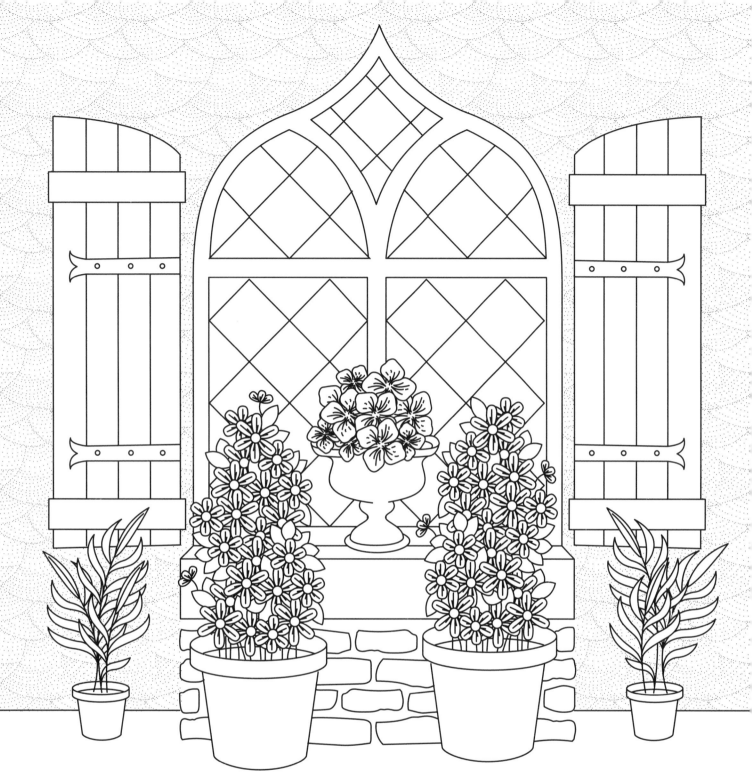

Better keep yourself clean
and bright; you are the
window through which
you must see the world.

GEORGE BERNARD SHAW

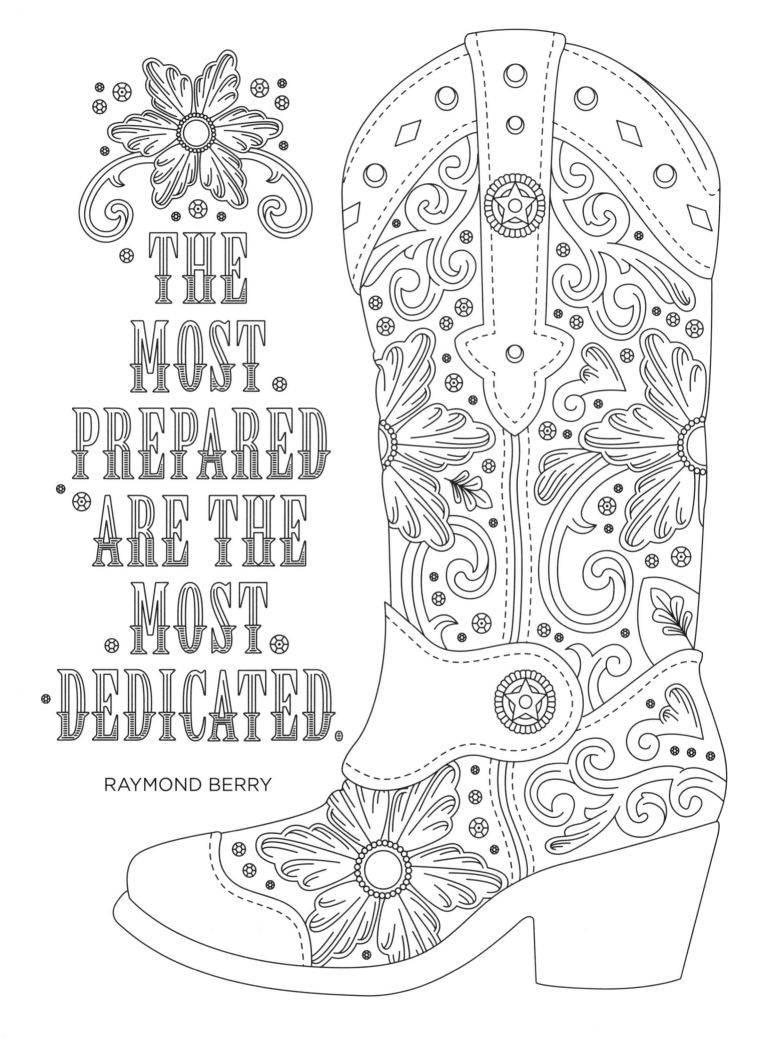

THE
MOST.
PREPARED
ARE THE
.MOST.
.DEDICATED.

RAYMOND BERRY

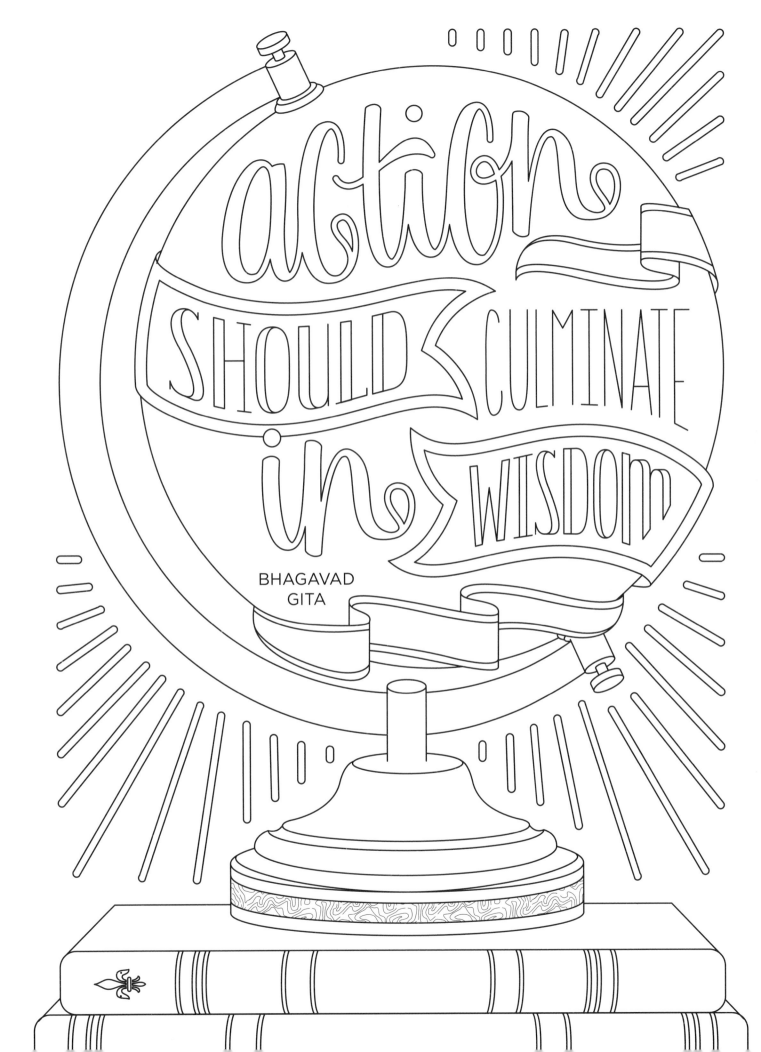

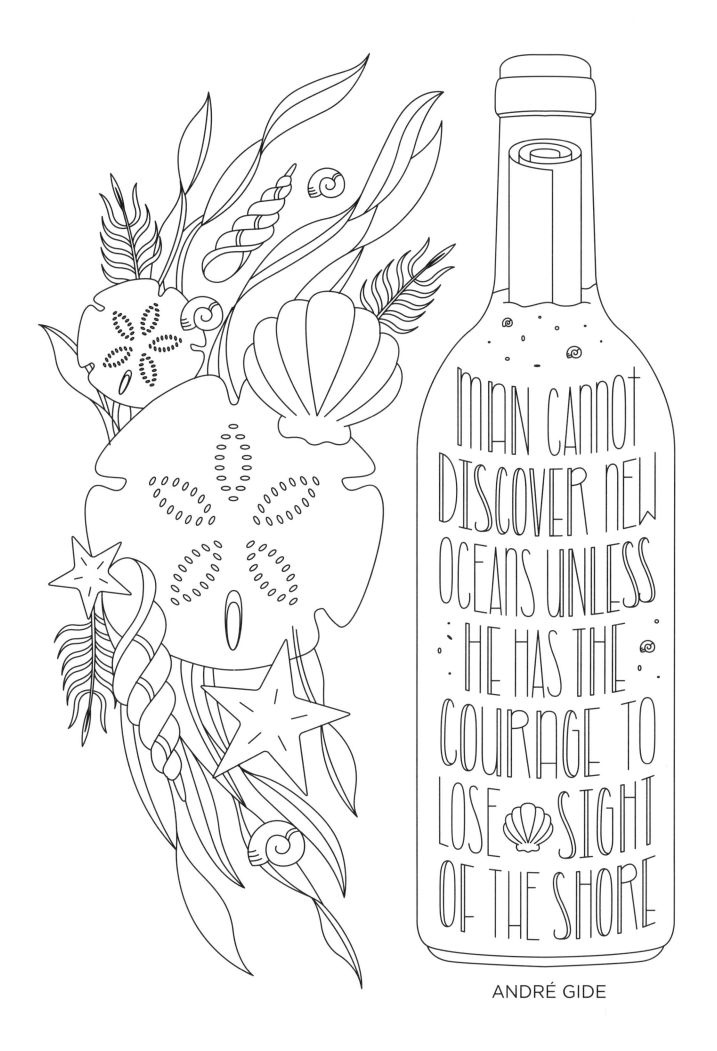

MAN CANNOT DISCOVER NEW OCEANS UNLESS HE HAS THE COURAGE TO LOSE SIGHT OF THE SHORE

ANDRÉ GIDE

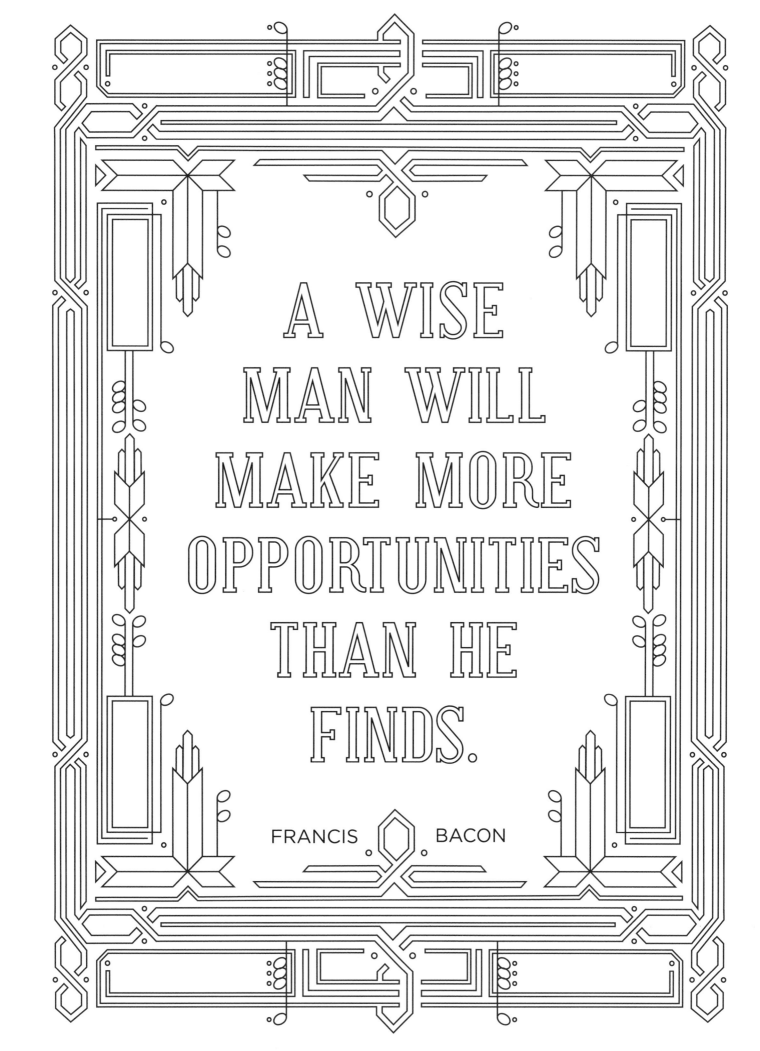

A WISE MAN WILL MAKE MORE OPPORTUNITIES THAN HE FINDS.

FRANCIS BACON

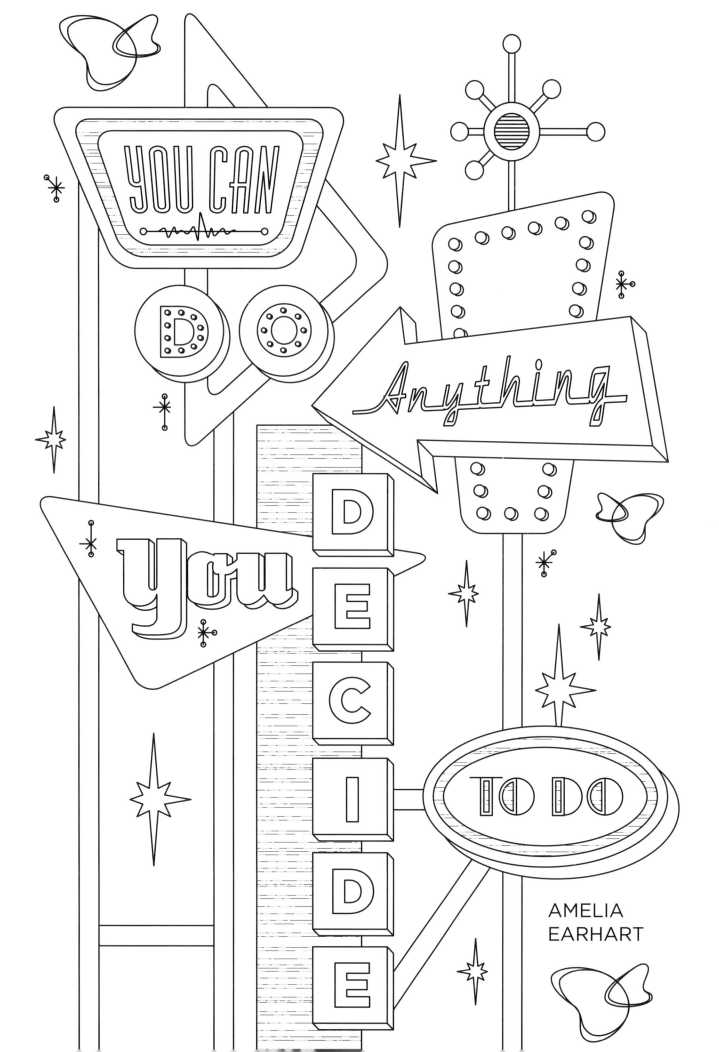

YOU CAN DO Anything You DECIDE TO DO

AMELIA EARHART

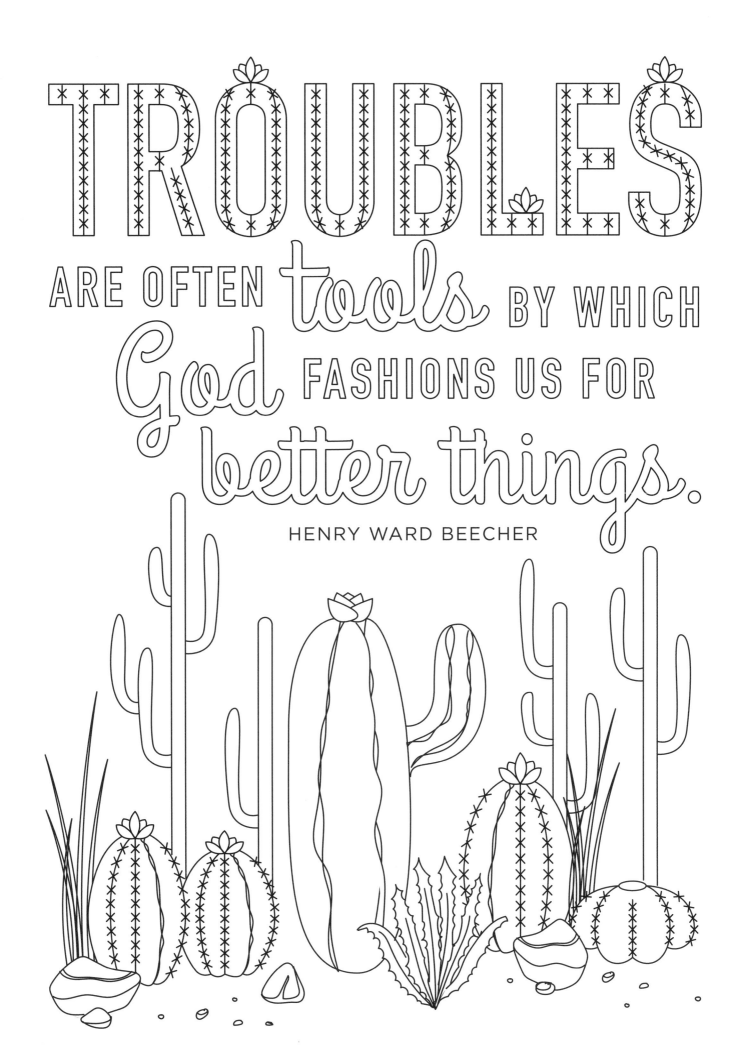

TROUBLES ARE OFTEN tools BY WHICH God FASHIONS US FOR better things.

HENRY WARD BEECHER

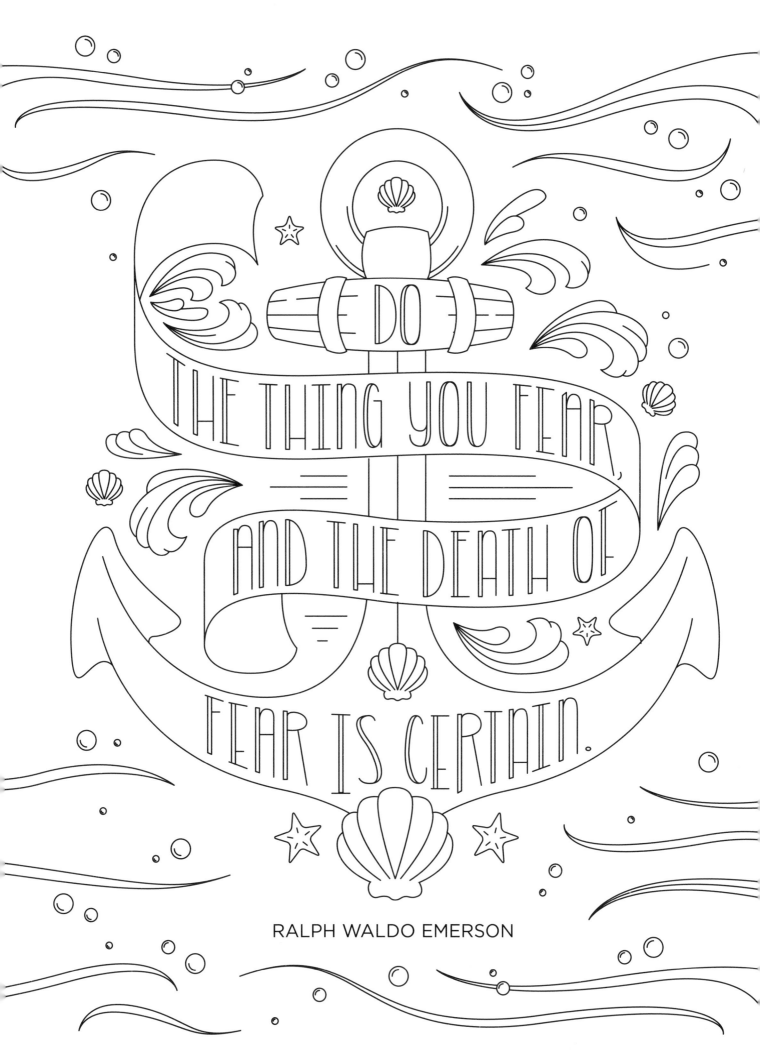

DO THE THING YOU FEAR, AND THE DEATH OF FEAR IS CERTAIN.

RALPH WALDO EMERSON

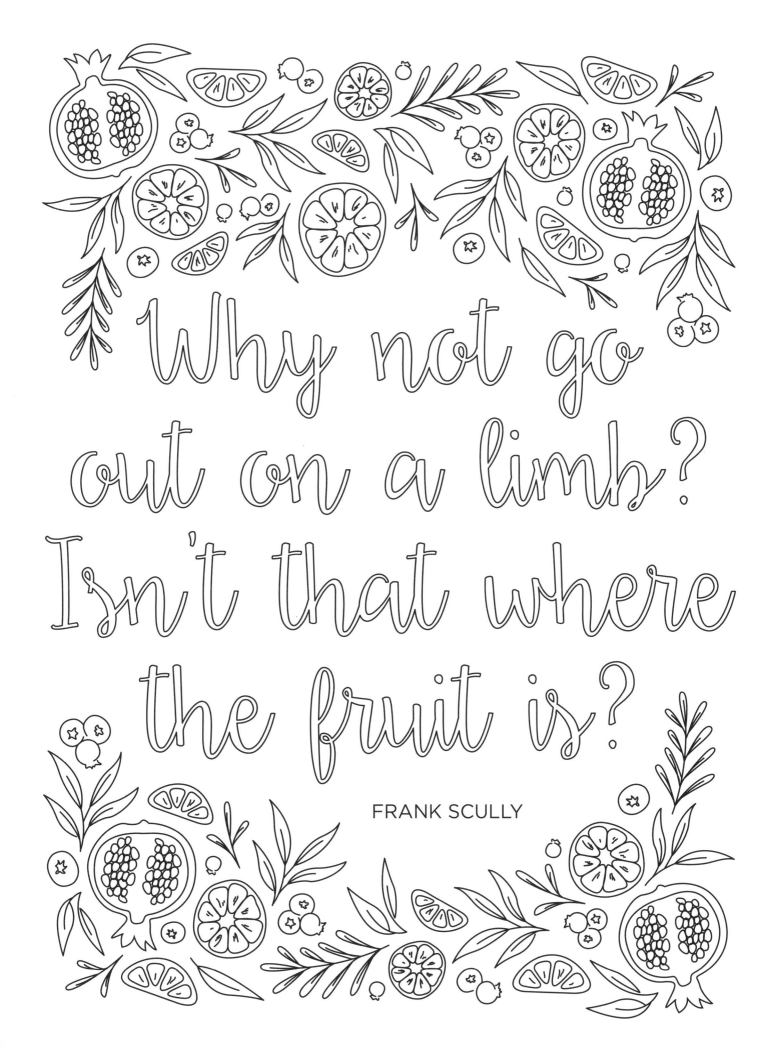

Why not go out on a limb? Isn't that where the fruit is?

FRANK SCULLY

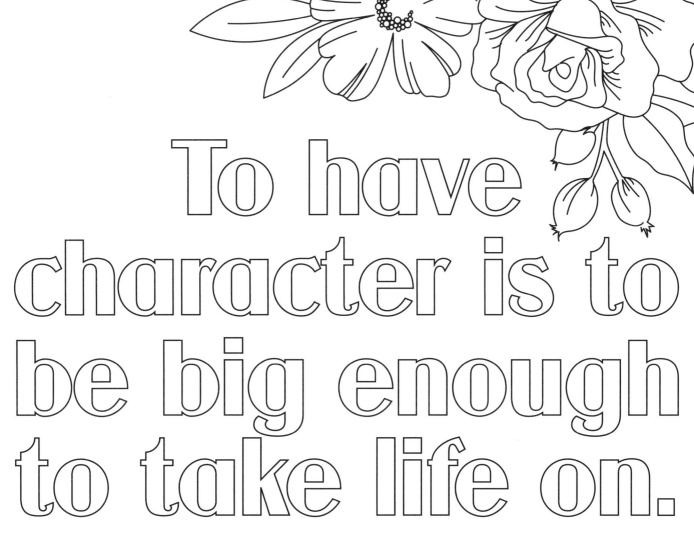

# To have character is to be big enough to take life on.

MARY CAROLINE RICHARDS

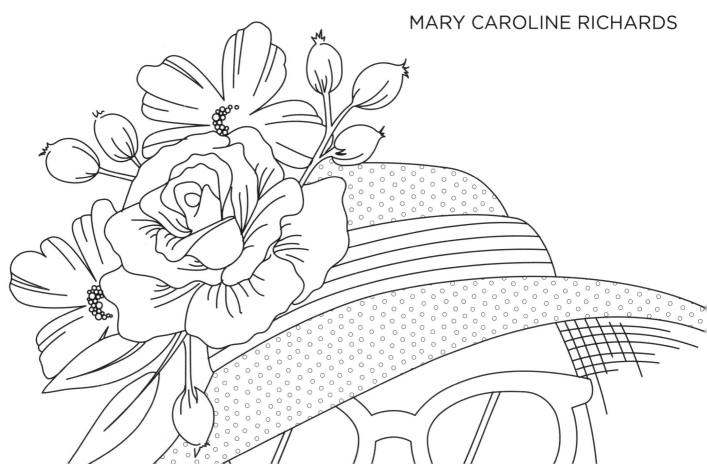

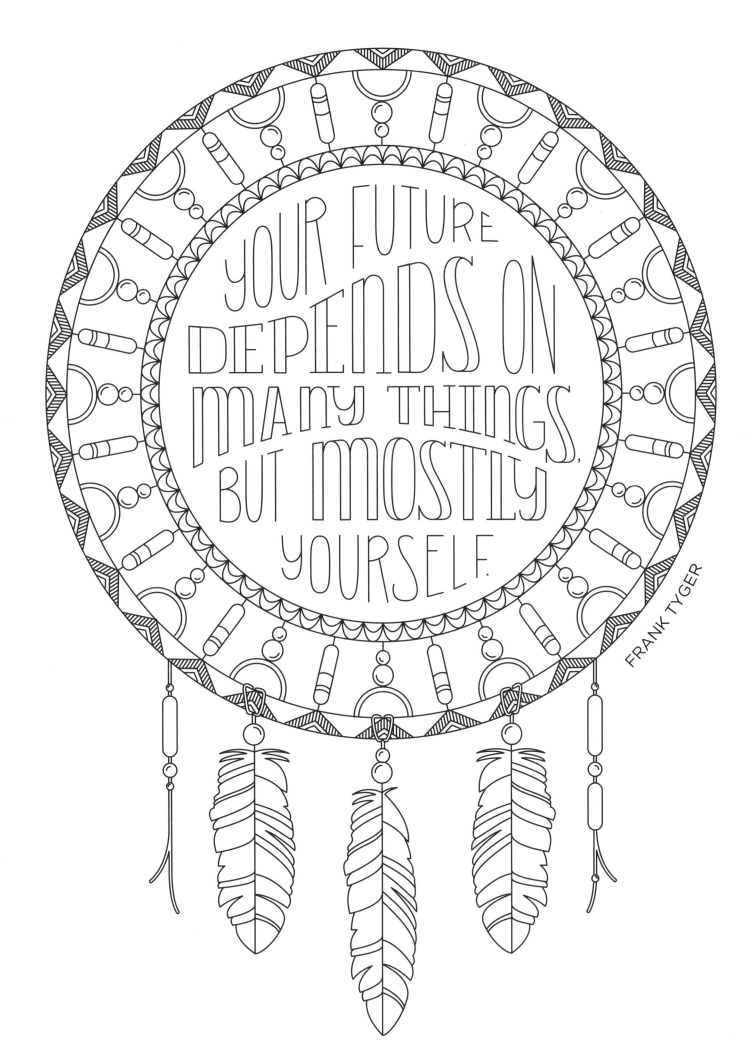

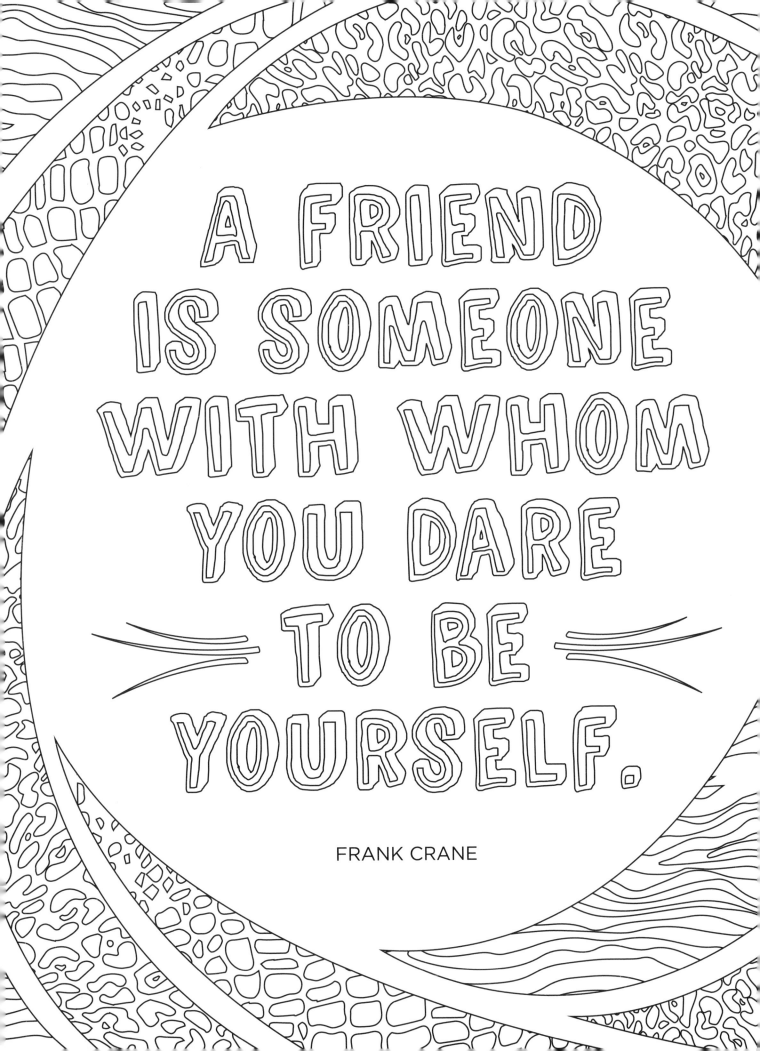

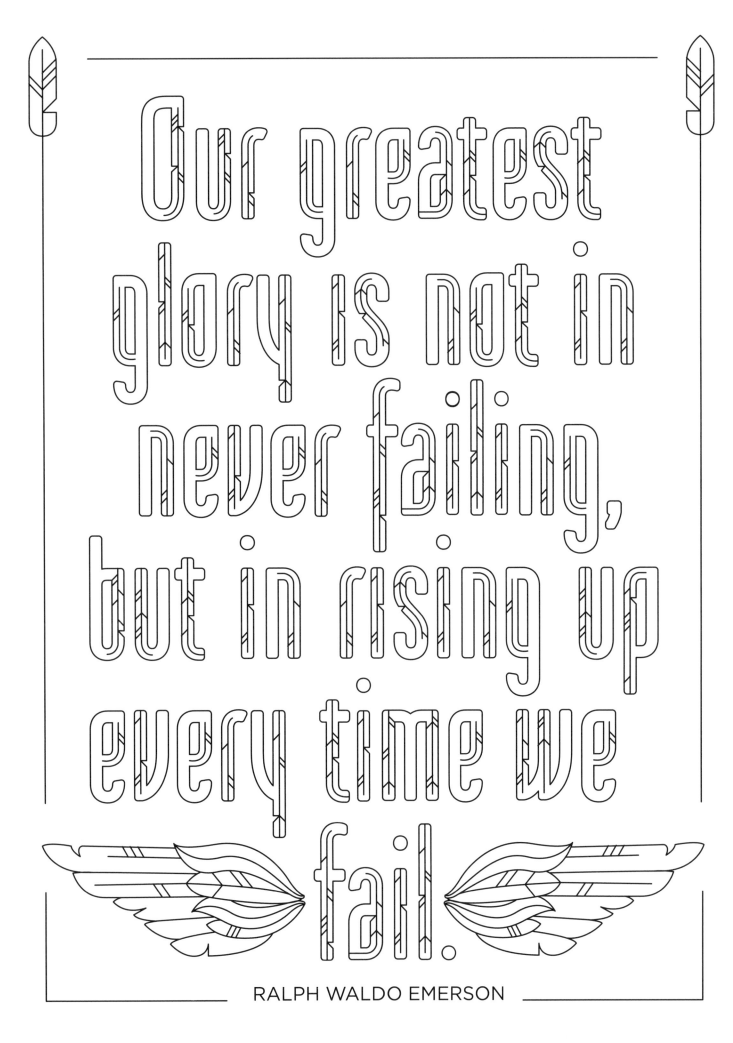

Our greatest glory is not in never failing, but in rising up every time we fail.

RALPH WALDO EMERSON

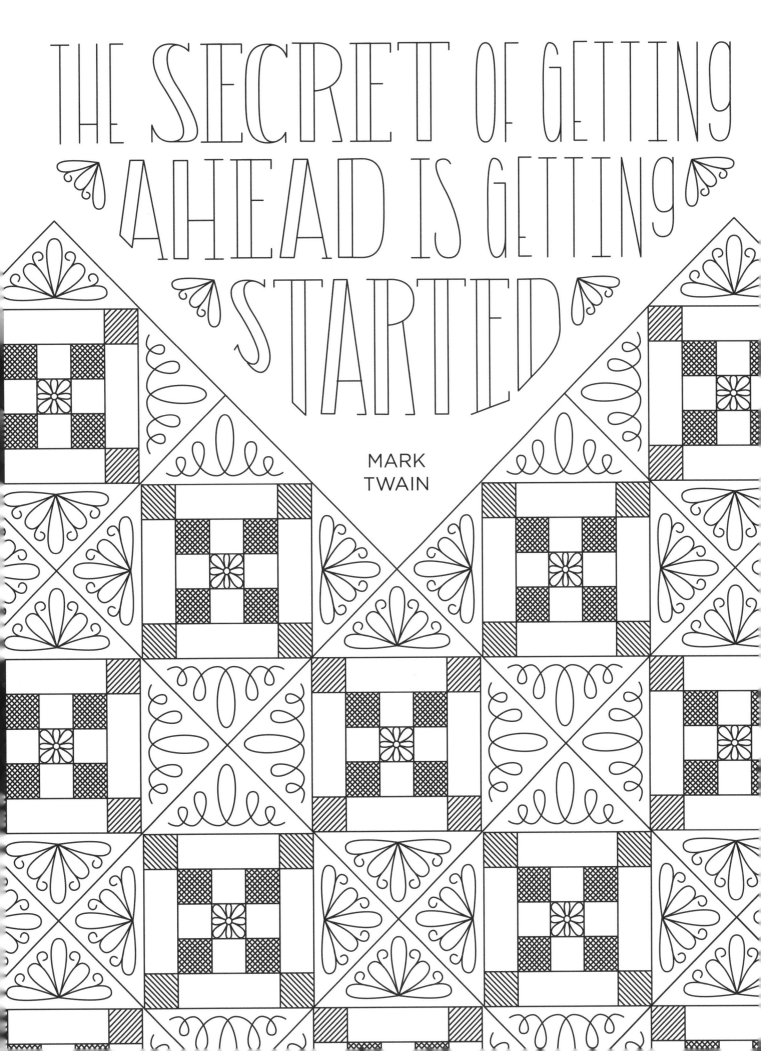

THE SECRET OF GETTING AHEAD IS GETTING STARTED

MARK TWAIN

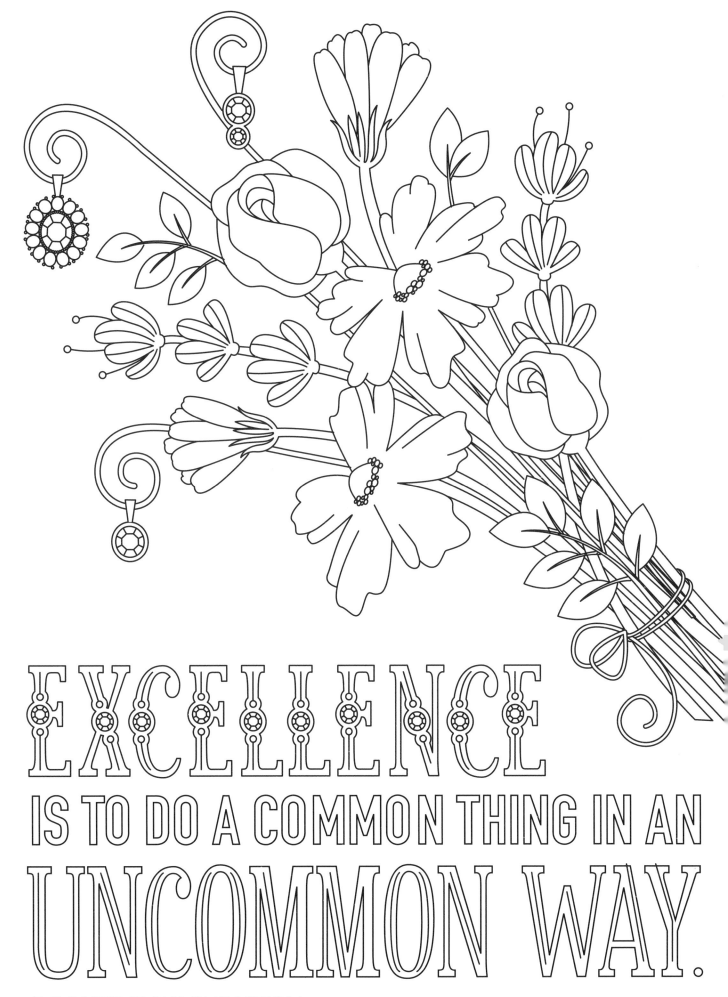

# EXCELLENCE
## IS TO DO A COMMON THING IN AN
# UNCOMMON WAY.

BOOKER T. WASHINGTON

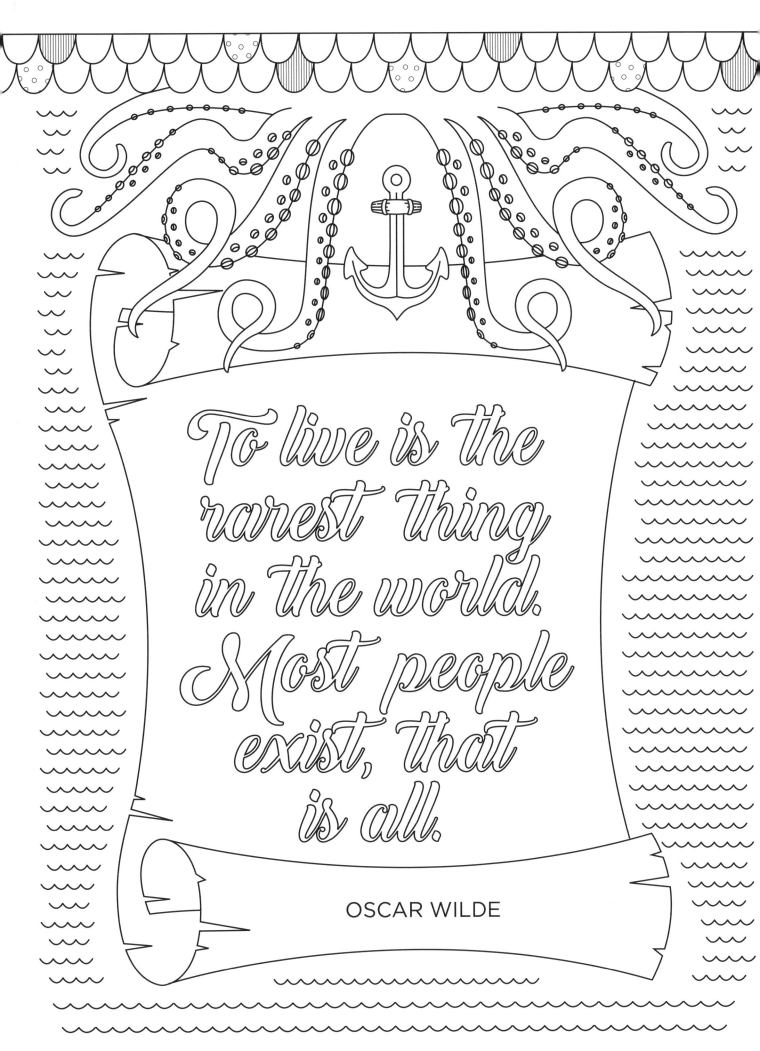

To live is the rarest thing in the world. Most people exist, that is all.

OSCAR WILDE

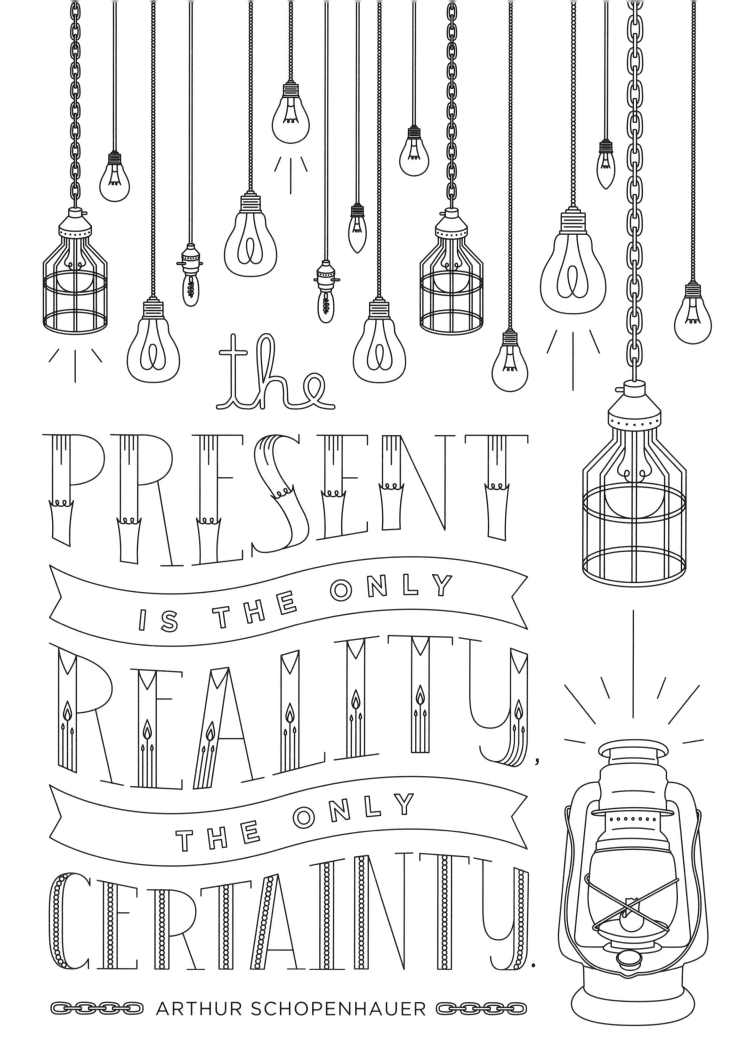

the PRESENT IS THE ONLY REALITY, THE ONLY CERTAINTY.

ARTHUR SCHOPENHAUER

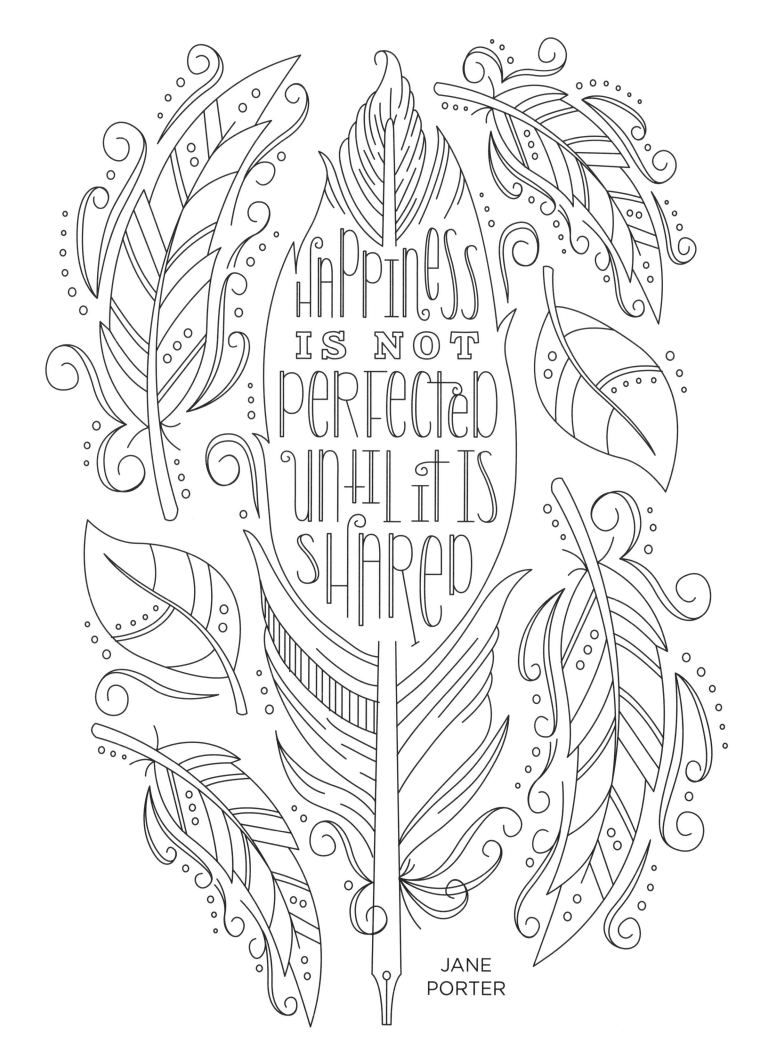

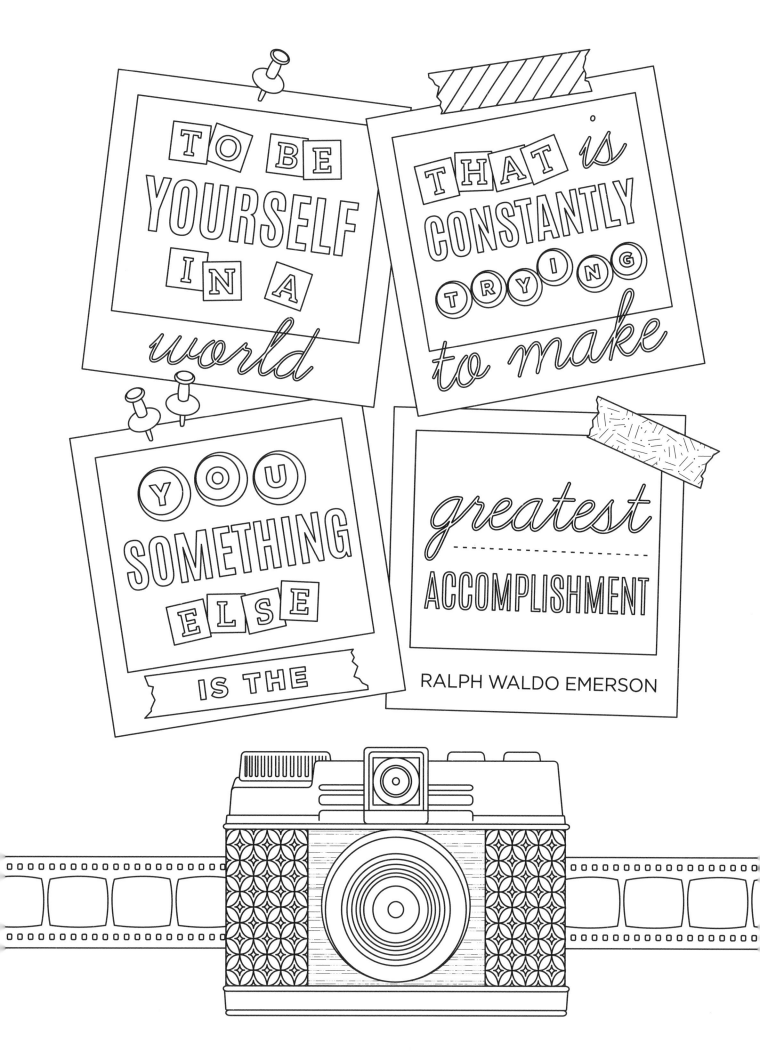

TO BE YOURSELF IN A *world*

THAT *is* CONSTANTLY TRYING to make

YOU SOMETHING ELSE IS THE

*greatest* ACCOMPLISHMENT

RALPH WALDO EMERSON

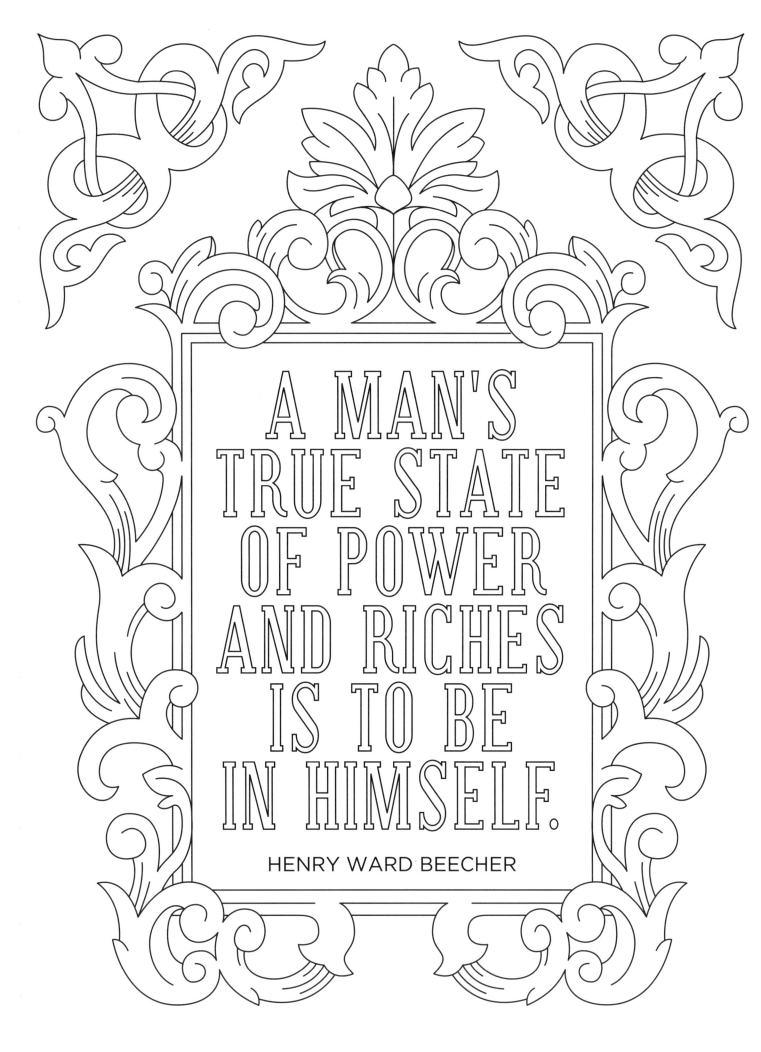

A MAN'S TRUE STATE OF POWER AND RICHES IS TO BE IN HIMSELF.

HENRY WARD BEECHER

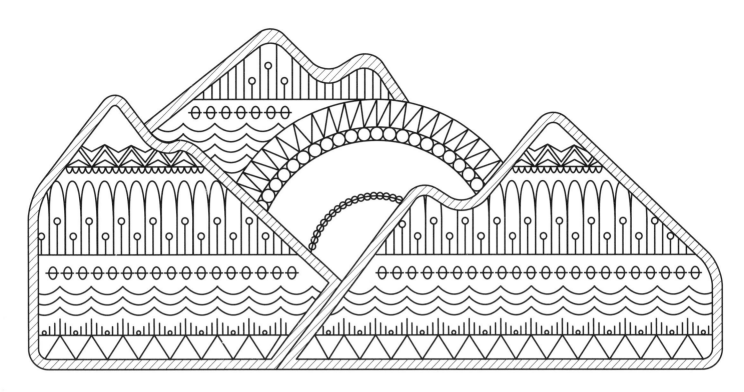

THE MAN WHO MOVES A MOUNTAIN BEGINS BY CARRYING AWAY SMALL STONES.

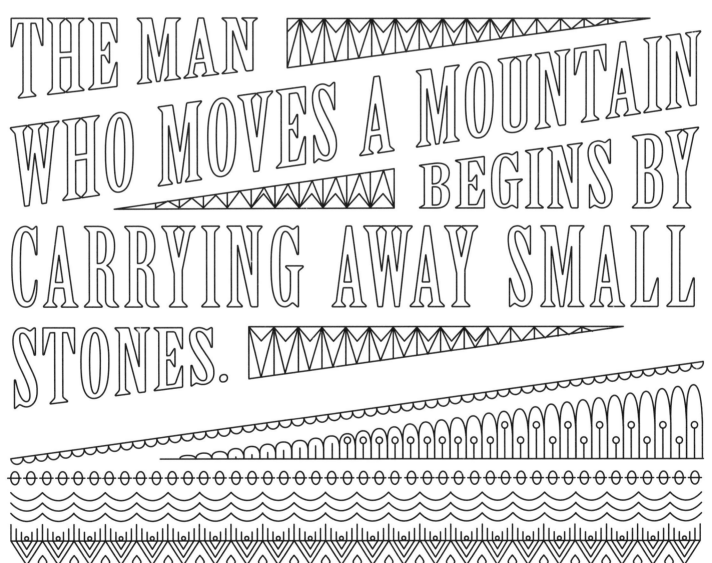

CONFUCIUS

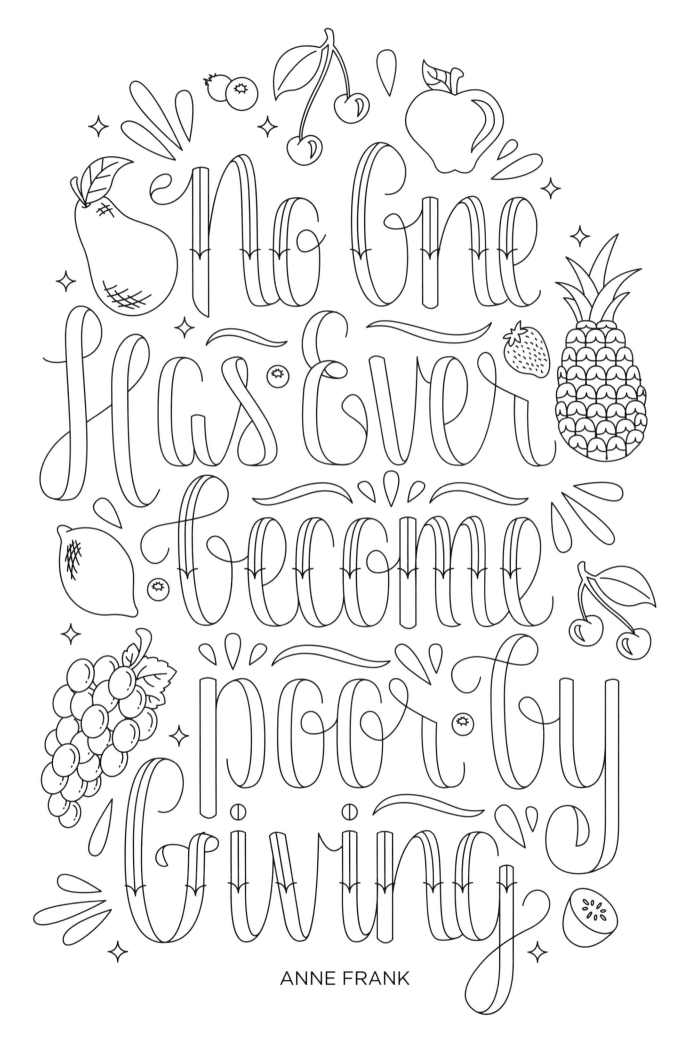

No One Has Ever Become Poor by Giving.

ANNE FRANK

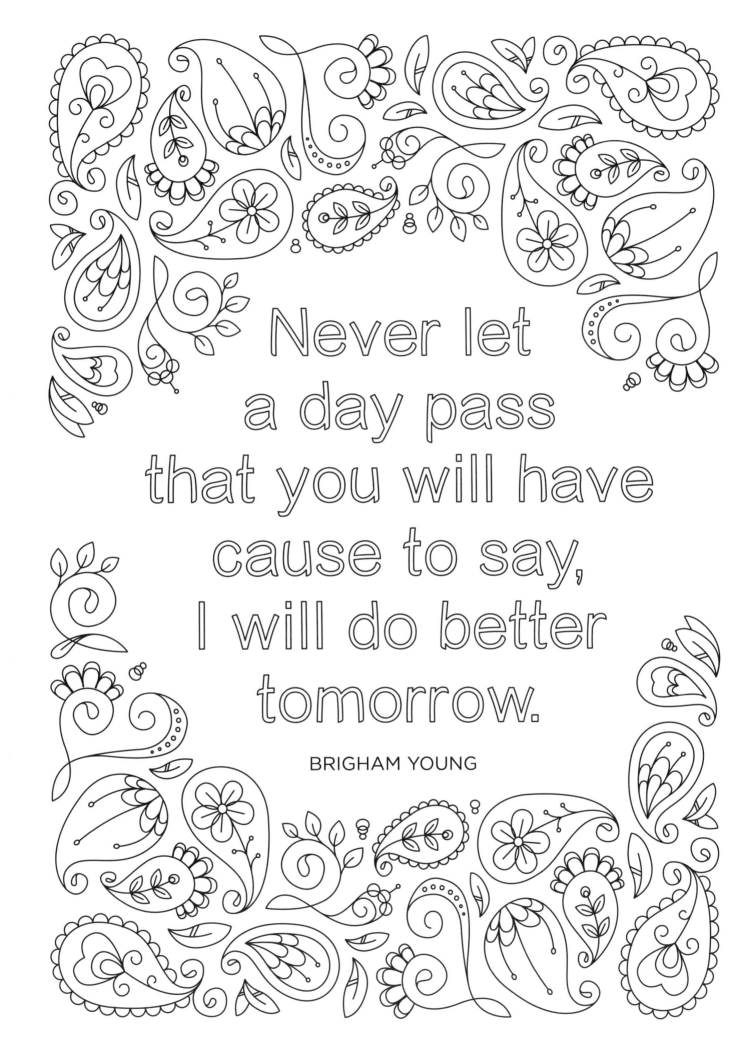

Never let a day pass that you will have cause to say, I will do better tomorrow.

BRIGHAM YOUNG

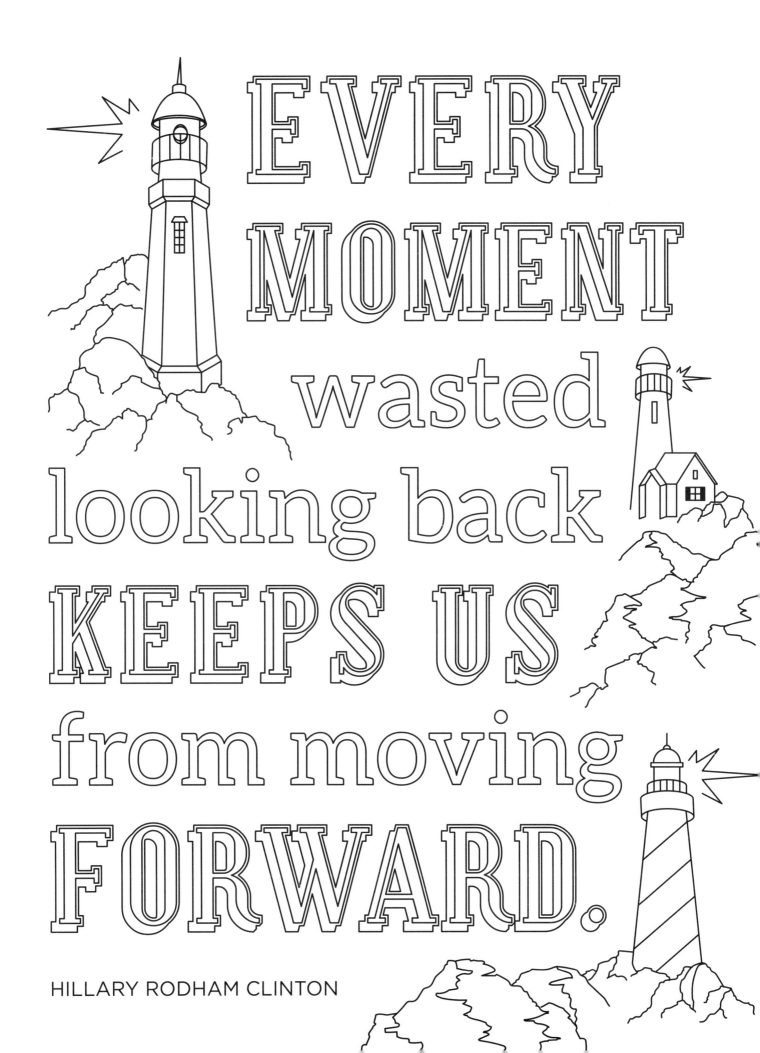

EVERY MOMENT wasted looking back KEEPS US from moving FORWARD.

HILLARY RODHAM CLINTON

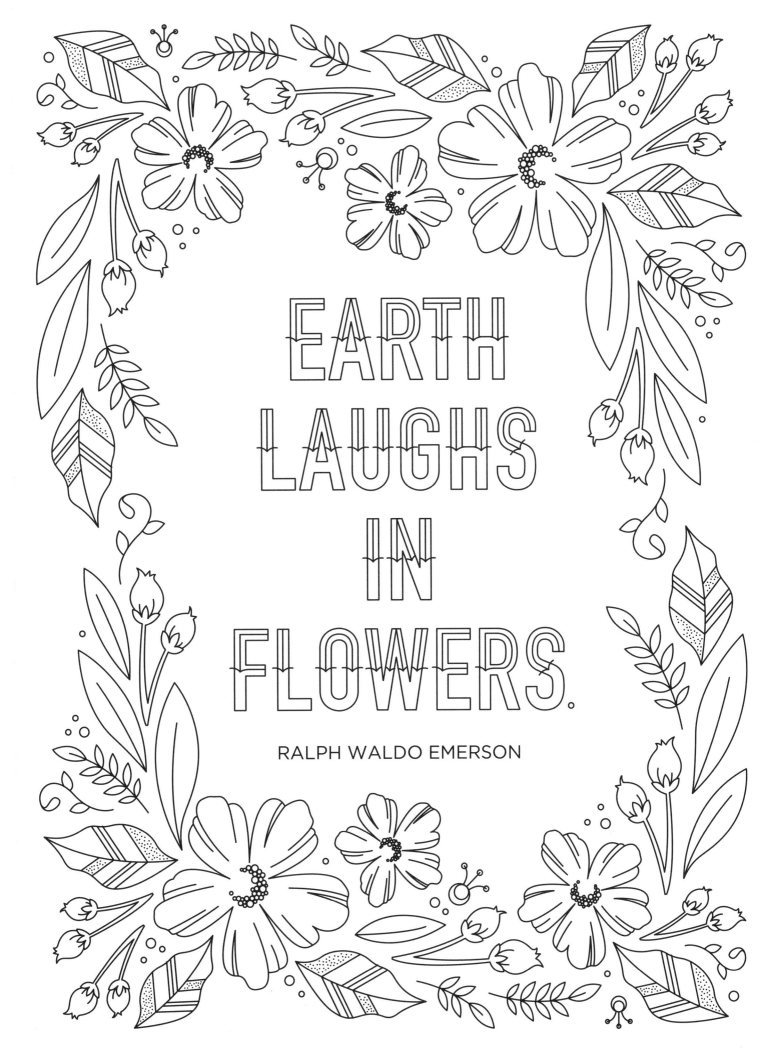

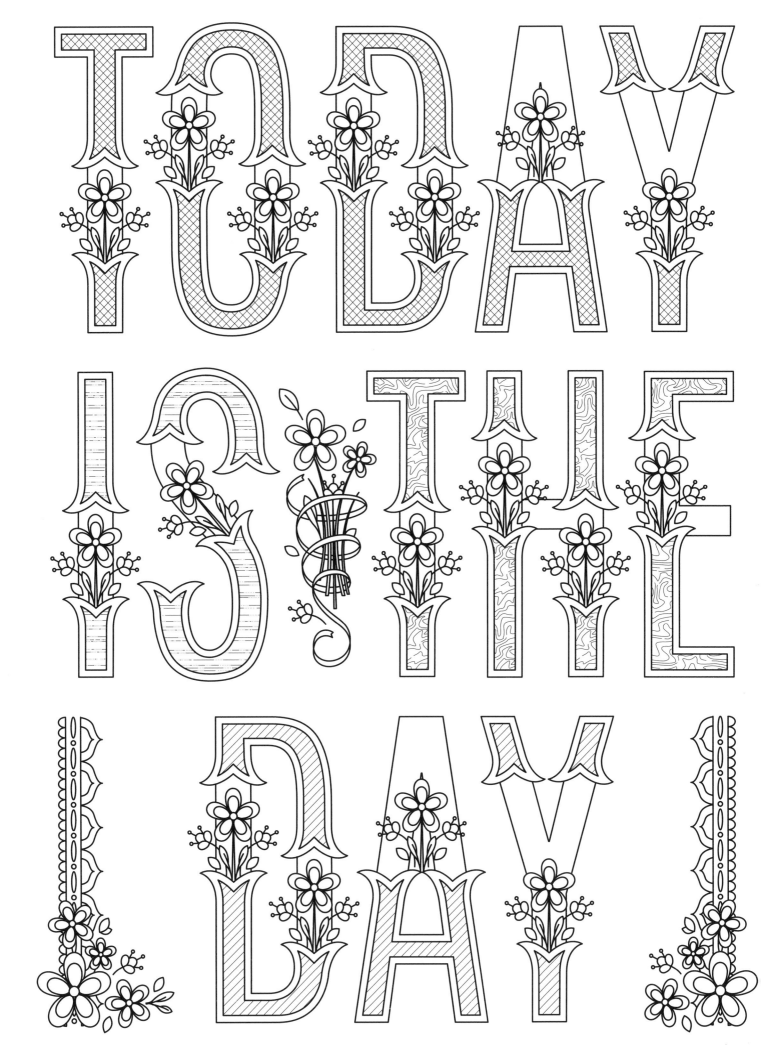

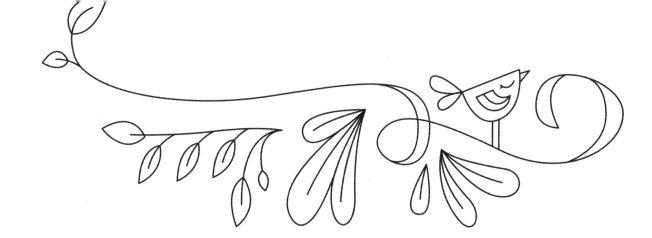

## ABOUT THE ILLUSTRATOR

Karlie Altherr has created successful branding and marketing campaigns for a wide variety of clients, including Microsoft and Lady Footlocker. She then started her own stationery business, Lighthouse Paper Co., where she designs greeting cards, notecards, and printed goods.

Published by Sourcebooks, Inc.
P.O. Box 4410, Naperville, Illinois 60567-4410
(630) 961-3900
Fax: (630) 961-2168
www.sourcebooks.com

Printed and bound in the United States of America.
VP 10 9 8 7 6 5 4 3 2 1